The BIG BOOK of WEEKEND CROCHET

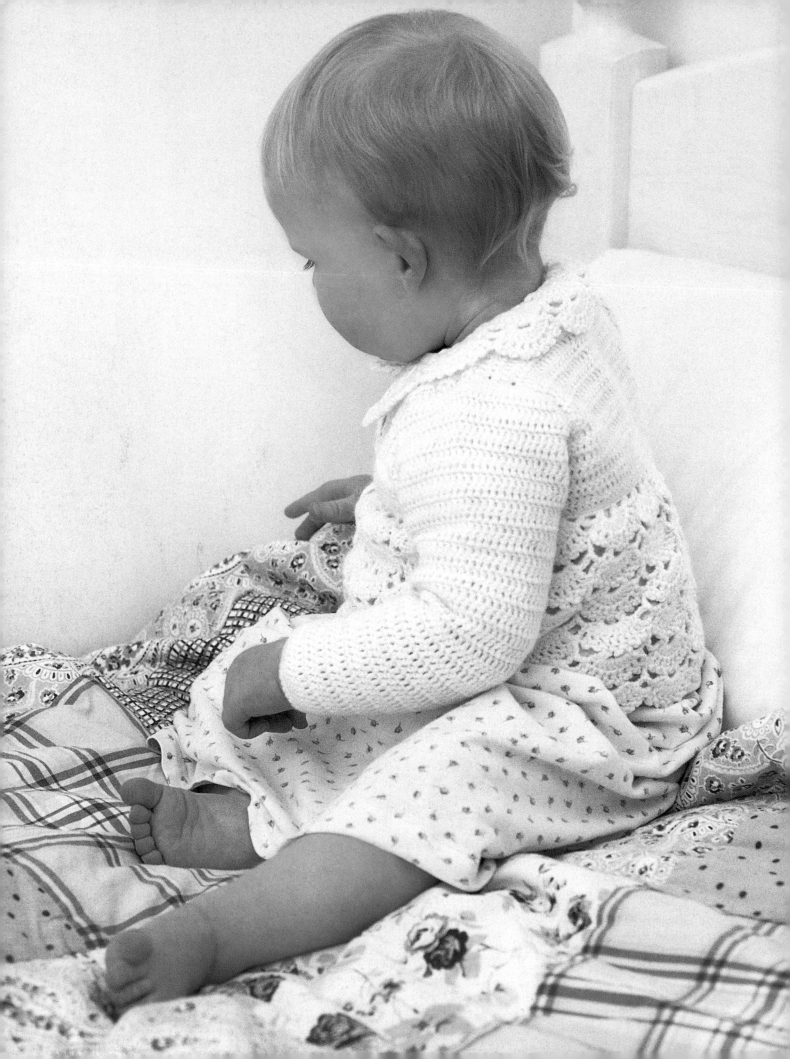

The **BIG BOOK** of WEEKEND CROCHET

Over 30 Stylish Projects—From Bags and Belts to Scarves and Wraps

Hilary Mackin and Sue Whiting

Reader's Digest

The Reader's Digest Association, Inc.
Pleasantville, New York/Montreal/Sydney

A READER'S DIGEST BOOK

This edition published by The Reader's Digest Association, Inc., by arrangement with New Holland Publishers (UK) Ltd.
Garfield House, 86–88 Edgware Road
London W2 2EA, United Kingdom
www.newhollandpublishers.com

Projects on front cover, clockwise from top: Fisherman's Sweater (page 118), Wraparound Jacket (page 78), Itty-bitty Cardigan (page 134), Tie-Front Bolero (page 71)
Projects on back cover, from top: Patchwork Cover-up (page 160), Lacy Openwork Tunic (page 50), Openwork Hip Hugger (page 90)

FOR NEW HOLLAND
Senior Editor: Clare Sayer
Design: Isobel Gillan
Photography: Sian Irvine
Production: Hazel Kirkman
Editorial Direction: Rosemary Wilkinson

FOR READER'S DIGEST
U.S. Project Editor: Marilyn J. Knowlton
Canadian Project Editor: Pamela Johnson
Technical Editor: Jane Townswick
Copy Editor: Barbara Booth
Associate Art Director: George McKeon
Executive Editor, Trade Publishing: Dolores York
Vice President and Publisher, Trade Publishing: Harold Clarke

ISBN-13: 978-0-7621-0696-7
ISBN-10: 0-7621-0696-4

Address any comments about **The Big Book of Weekend Crochet** to:

The Reader's Digest Association, Inc.
Adult Trade Publishing
Reader's Digest Road
Pleasantville, NY 10570-7000

For more Reader's Digest products and information, visit our website:

www.rd.com (in the United States)
www.readersdigest.ca (in Canada)
www.readersdigest.com.au (in Australia)
www.readersdigest.com.nz (in New Zealand)

Reproduction by Pica Digital PTE Ltd, Singapore
Printing and binding by Times Offset, Malaysia

1 3 5 7 9 10 8 6 4 2 (paperback)

CONTENTS

INTRODUCTION

In recent years crochet has become as popular as knitting—both crafts made more interesting due to the wonderful yarns available as well as the current fashion trends, which include accessories such as boleros, shrugs, capelets, and scarves. They not only look stunning, they are also comfortable to wear.

To do crochet, you need to grasp just a few basic easy stitches. All pattern stitches are variations on these basic stitches, providing interesting textures and different looks. Crocheting can be done just about anywhere, so slip it into your bag if you have a train journey or bus ride, or do it while waiting for an appointment. The onlookers will be fascinated by your expertise and dexterity and astonished at how quickly the work grows.

The possibilities are endless—with just a hook and some yarn, you can create anything from a delicate lacy tunic to a warm jacket. Using some of the wonderful specialist yarns available, you can also create some stunning accessories, from shimmery scarves to hats and bags. Making items for babies and children is a real joy, because there is such a wonderful range of soft and colorful yarns to choose from. And once your wardrobe is complete, you can begin to transform your home with some wonderful crocheted pieces, such as a stylish bedspread, a colorful throw, or a fun faux-fur rug and pillows.

This book includes some simple patterns aimed at the beginner, but also more complex patterns for those who prefer something a little more challenging. So give it a try; you'll soon be "hooked" on this fun, rewarding, and fashionable craft!

Getting started

Crochet is incredibly versatile, and the beauty of this wonderful craft is that you can achieve such varying effects with the simplest of materials. All you really need to get started is a crochet hook and a ball of yarn. In this section, you will find all the information you need to follow a pattern successfully.

CROCHET HOOKS

Available in a wide range of sizes, crochet hooks are graded by several different systems. The simplest system is the metric one, which is used in Europe and is now becoming familiar in the United States. Metrically sized hooks range from a tiny 0.60 mm (a little narrower than a pin) up to a chunky 15 mm (⅝ in.). Medium- to large-size American hooks—referred to as "regular" and "jiffy" (in the case of large ones)—are graded by letter and/or number (the latter corresponding to knitting needle sizes), with the size increasing along with the number or rank in the alphabet. The smallest is a B/1 (about 2.00 mm), and the largest are graded Q or S (about 16 and 19 mm, respectively). These medium-to-large hooks and their metric equivalents are commonly made of aluminum, plastic, or less often, wood, bamboo, or bone. Small American hooks, made of steel, are sized in reverse numerical order, from 00 (a little over 3.00 mm) down to a minuscule 14 (about 0.60 mm).

Extra-long crochet hooks are used for Tunisian crochet (also called afghan stitch); some of these have a hook at each end of the shank for making double-faced, two-color fabrics.

The table opposite shows metric and U.S. equivalent sizes. Please note, however, that the equivalents are not usually exact and there are even slight variations between American manufacturers. If you cannot obtain the correct gauge (see page 12) using an American hook, you might do better with the metric equivalent; see the Internet for sources of these.

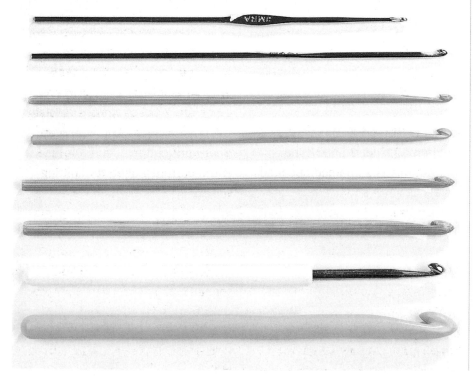

Crochet hooks come in many sizes.

CROCHET HOOK CONVERSION CHART

Steel hooks

U.S.	METRIC (mm)
14	0.60
12	0.75
10	1.00
8	1.25
7	1.50
5	1.75

Aluminum or acrylic hooks (wood or bamboo)

U.S.	METRIC (mm)
B/1	2.00
C/2	2.50
D/3	3.25
E/4	3.50
F/5	3.75
G/6	4.25
7	4.50
H/8	5.00
I/9	5.50
J/10	6.00
K/10	7.00
L/11	8.00
M/13	9.00
N/15	10.00

YARNS

Traditional crochet consisted almost exclusively of delicate openwork designs made of very fine crochet cotton (smooth and tightly twisted), worked with tiny steel hooks. This form of crochet was used mainly for household objects, such as place mats, dressing-table sets, and tablecloths. It was also used to embellish clothing with lacy collars and cuffs. It is not advisable for the beginner to attempt such intricate work.

Today crochet is used mainly for clothing and for sturdier household accessories, and the range of yarns available for this kind of work is enormous. In addition to American yarns, there is a host of imported yarns. All of these are designated by different terms—some relating to the thickness, or "weights," of the yarn, some to its construction, some to its traditional use. As you gain experience in crochet, you'll become familiar with these terms. Here are some of the most common:

Knitting worsted (U.S.), a relatively heavy, smooth wool yarn; "worsted weight" describes a similar yarn spun from synthetic or a blend of natural and synthetic fibers.

Double knitting/DK (British, Continental), finer than knitting worsted, this is so named because it is about twice as thick as "four-ply" yarn (see below), although it, too, is spun from four plies, or strands.

Sport weight (U.S.), a medium-weight yarn, somewhat lighter than double knitting.

Four-ply (U.K.), a little lighter than sport weight. Note that many other yarns, including knitting worsted, have four plies; the name of this yarn identifies its particular weight.

You'll also encounter **fisherman** (U.S.)/**Aran** (U.K.) yarns, which are smooth yarns about the same weight as knitting worsted; **bulky/chunky** yarns, and fine **fingering** (U.S.) and **two-ply Shetland yarns** (U.K.), which are often used for lacy patterns. Novelty yarns come in a huge range of weights, textures, and colors, including multicolored effects.

Many of today's crocheted fashions use thick yarns, both smooth and textured, which are quick and easy to work, especially using an oversized hook and an openwork pattern. As a rule, the yarns currently used for knitting are equally suited for crochet, although bouclé and nubby yarns can be difficult to handle, especially in patterns requiring several stitches to be worked together. A smooth yarn will show off the stitch pattern well, and one that is tightly twisted will give a firm finish. For a soft, fluffy effect, choose a long-haired yarn.

Choosing yarns

All the patterns in this book specify the yarn to be used, and for the best results it is advisable to use this recommended yarn. If you cannot find this yarn, choose one of similar weight and type; also make sure that the total length of the substitute yarn is at least as long as the total length of the original yarn. Many yarn labels give the length in the ball (if not, ask the salesperson); multiply this by the number of balls required and do the same for the recommended yarn. Make a gauge swatch (see page 12) to check that the crochet will be the correct size.

Yarns used in this book

(Lengths per ball are approximate, depending on the dye, and the weights in ounces are approximate conversions of the total grams—the system of measurement used for these imported yarns.)

Colinette Graffiti: 100% wool; 87 yds. (80 m) per 100-g (3½-oz.) hank

Colinette Lasso: 100% polyamide; 224 yds. (205 m) per 100-g (3½-oz.) hank

Colinette Tagliatelle: 90% merino wool, 10% nylon; 158 yds. (145 m) per 100-g (3½-oz.) hank

Lion Brand Boucle: 79% acrylic, 20% mohair, 1% nylon; 57 yds. (52 m) per 70-g (2½-oz.) ball

Lion Brand Cotton: 100% cotton; 236 yds. (212 m) per 140-g (5-oz.) ball

Lion Brand Jiffy: 100% acrylic; 135 yds. (123 m) per 85-g (3-oz.) ball

Lion Brand Micro Spun: 100% microfiber acrylic; 168 yds. (154 m) per 70-g (2½-oz.) ball

Rowan 4-ply Cotton: 100% cotton; 186 yds. (170 m) per 50-g (1¾-oz.) ball

Rowan Calmer: 75% cotton, 25% acrylic/microfiber; 175 yds. (160 m) per 50-g (1¾-oz.) ball

Rowan Cashsoft Baby DK: 57% extra-fine merino, 33% microfiber, 10% cashmere; 142 yds. (130 m) per 50-g (1¾-oz.) ball

Rowan Cash Cotton DK: 35% cotton, 25% polyamide, 18% angora, 13% viscose, 9% cashmere; 142 yds. (130 m) per 50-g (1¾-oz.) ball

Rowan Cotton Glace: 100% cotton; 126 yds. (115 m) per 50-g (1¾-oz.) ball

Rowan Handknit Cotton DK: 100% cotton; 93 yds. (85 m) per 50-g (1¾-oz.) ball

Rowan Kid Classic: 70% lambswool, 26% kid mohair, 4% nylon; 153 yds. (140 m) per 50-g (1¾-oz.) ball

Rowan Soft Baby: Wool blends; 150 m per 50-g (1¾-oz.) ball

Rowan Summer Tweed: 70% silk, 30% cotton; 118 yds. (108 m) per 50-g (1¾-oz.) hank

Sirdar Breeze DK: 60% acrylic, 40% cotton; 28 yds. (26 m) per 100-g (3½-oz.) ball

Sirdar Cotton DK: 100% cotton; 184 yds. (169 m) per 100-g (3½-oz.) ball

Sirdar Country Style DK: 45% acrylic, 40% nylon, 15% wool; 347 yds. (318 m) per 100-g (3½-oz.) ball

Sirdar Foxy: 100% polyester; 98 yds. (90 m) per 50-g (1¾-oz.) ball

Sirdar Funky Fur: 100% polyester; 98 yds. (90 m) per 50-g (1¾-oz.) ball

Sirdar Silky Look DK: 93% acrylic, 7% nylon; 147 yds. (135 m) per 50-g (1¾-oz.) ball

Sirdar Snuggly DK: 55% nylon, 45% acrylic; 98 yds. (90 m) per 50-g (1¾-oz.) ball

Sirdar Snuggly 4-ply: 55% nylon, 45% acrylic; 98 yds. (90 m) per 50-g (1¾-oz.) ball

Sirdar Tuscany: 57% polyester, 38% acrylic, 5% nylon; 62 yds. (57 m) per 50-g (1¾-oz.) ball

Sirdar Wash 'n' Wear: 55% nylon, 45% acrylic; 347 yds. (318 m) per 100-g (3½-oz.) ball

Twilleys Freedom Cotton: 100% cotton; 93 yds. (85 m) per 50-g (1¾-oz.) ball

OTHER ESSENTIALS

Tapestry needles These blunt-pointed needles with large eyes are used for sewing seams; a sharp-pointed needle might split the yarn and weaken it. The oversized eye allows for easy threading.

Tape measure Use a good-quality tape measure that won't stretch; accurate measurements are important when checking gauge.

Pins Use long pins with large heads for holding pieces together prior to seaming; these are less likely to get lost in the crochet.

Scissors Have a sharp pair on hand for cutting lengths of yarn.

FOLLOWING PATTERNS AND SIZING

Before beginning a pattern, it is important to check a few things so that you won't be disappointed with the end result.

Check the "actual" measurements given with the pattern. Depending on the style of the garment, there may be less or more ease than you prefer for the fit you require. If in doubt, measure one of your favorite garments and compare its measurements to those given with the pattern.

It is best to read the whole pattern before starting to crochet. This gives a valuable overall picture of how the stitch pattern works and how the whole article is put together.

Most of the patterns for garments in this book give more than one size. The instructions are given for the smallest size first, with figures for the larger size(s) following in parentheses ( ). Where the figure "0" appears, no stitches or rows are to be worked in that particular size. Where there is only one set of figures given, this applies to all sizes.

Work the figures in brackets [ ] the number of times stated after the second bracket; for example, "[ch 1, skip 1 ch, 1 dc into next st] 5 times." Brackets can also be used to clarify working a number of stitches into one stitch: for example, "[1 tr, ch 3, 1 tr] into next st." Stitch counts are also given throughout the patterns, at the end of a row; this helps you to check that the number of increasing and decreasing stitches is correct.

Asterisks are used to indicate a repetition of instructions. The whole sequence between the asterisk and the next semicolon is to be repeated as many times as necessary to reach the end of the row; for example, "* ch 1, skip 1 ch, 1 tr into next st, ch 1, skip 1 ch, 1 tr into each of next 3 sts; rep from * to end, turn."

ABBREVIATIONS

Abbreviations are used for many of the repetitive words that occur in patterns (see below). Abbreviations that are specific to a pattern will be given with the rest of the pattern information.

Common abbreviations
alt = alternate
approx = approximate(ly)
beg = begin(ning)
cm = centimeter(s)
cont = continue
foll = following

in. = inch(es)
mm = millimeter(s)
rem = remaining
rep = repeat
RS = right side
tog = together
WS = wrong side

Crochet terms and abbreviations
ch = chain(s)
ch sp = chain space
cl = cluster
dec = decrease
dc = double crochet
dtr = double triple
gr = group
hdc = half double crochet
inc = increase
quadtr = quadruple triple
quintr = quintuple triple

sc = single crochet

ss = slip stitch

stch = starting ch

st(s) = stitch(es)

tch = turning chain

tr = triple

ttr = triple triple

yoh = yarn over hook

Base (foundation) chain The length of chain made at the beginning of a piece of crochet as a basis for constructing the fabric. It is made up of a number of chain stitches.

Turning/starting chain One or more chains, depending on the length of the stitch required, worked at the beginning of a row (or end of the last row). This sometimes counts as the first stitch on a new row (starting chain) when working in rounds.

GAUGE

Probably the most important factor in making a successful garment is to obtain the correct gauge. This is the number of stitches or rows worked over a given measurement.

Checking the gauge.

Often we are so eager to get on with our crocheting, we assume that our gauge will be correct. The gauge is governed not only by the size of the yarn and hook but also by the tension with which one works. (For this reason, gauge is called "tension" in Britain.) It is worth spending a little time to get the gauge right, because too loose a gauge will produce a larger garment, and the fabric will be too floppy to hold its shape; you could also run out of yarn. Too tight a gauge would produce a smaller garment, and the fabric will be too stiff.

The best way to check your gauge is to make up a swatch of crochet fabric about 6 in. (15 cm) square, using the yarn and hook size that are recommended in the pattern and working the stitch pattern for the design as stated at the beginning of the pattern. Lay this on a flat surface, being careful not to stretch it. Using long pins, mark out the gauge measurement given in the pattern—usually 4 in. (10 cm)—in both directions. Count the number of stitches and rows within this area, remembering to include any half stitches. If you have too few stitches and rows, your work is too loose and you should try a smaller hook. If you have too many stitches and rows, your work is too tight; try a larger hook. Work another gauge swatch and measure again. Repeat, if necessary, until you have the correct gauge.

Where a pattern uses different sizes of hook in one garment, you will have to adjust all the hooks in the same way.

Note The hook size suggested in the pattern is only a guide. You must use whichever hook gives you the correct gauge.

Hint Stitch gauge is generally more important than row gauge because a pattern normally instructs you to work until you reach a certain length; therefore, the number of rows within that length can vary slightly without affecting the size. The number of stitches, however, is dictated by the pattern, so their size will govern the width of the garment.

PRESSING AND BLOCKING

Always read the manufacturer's instructions on the yarn label to see if pressing is recommended and, if so, what iron temperature is advised. The label will also give any care instructions. If any pressing is necessary, it is best to press on the wrong side of the work. Cover the item with a clean cloth before pressing. Note that pressing is different from ironing. You do not slide the iron over the surface, but lower it onto the fabric for a second or two and then lift it away.

When a piece of crochet fabric is very textured, it is sometimes better to block the item rather than press it. For blocking, use a clean, flat surface into which you can stick dressmaker's pins, such as an ironing board. Pin the piece out to the correct measurements. Cover it with a damp cloth and leave it to dry.

Crochet techniques

Once you have mastered the basic stitches, you can go on to create a whole range of wonderful crochet pieces. Discover how to work longer stitches, work increases and decreases, and create decorative effects. Finally, learn how to finish your crochet items for a professional look.

MAKING A SLIP KNOT

Almost all crochet begins with a base or starting chain, which is a series of chain stitches beginning with a slip knot.

Make a slip loop about 6 in. (15 cm) from the cut end of yarn. Slip this over the crochet hook and pull up the end so the loop sits comfortably around the crochet hook, just below the actual hook section.

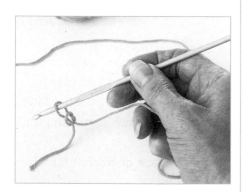

Making a slip loop.

Note for left-handers Work from these photographs, but use a mirror so that the diagrams are a "mirror image" (in reverse); read the text from the book, replacing "left" for "right" and "right" for "left" where applicable.

HOLDING THE HOOK

Hold the hook in your right hand (left hand if you're left-handed) in the same way as a pencil, with the thumb and forefinger over the flat section of the hook.

Holding the hook (pencil grip).

Alternatively, you can hold it in a firmer, overhand grip.

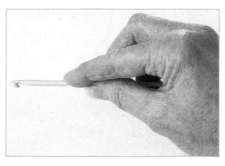

Holding the hook (overhand grip).

HOLDING THE YARN AND WORK

The left hand holds the work and controls the yarn. Try to keep the grip of the thumb and first finger of the right hand near the new stitch; this helps to keep the gauge correct.

Once the first loop is on the hook, wind the yarn once around the little finger, then over the third, middle, and index fingers. Use the index finger to manipulate the yarn as you work, and the middle finger and thumb to hold the work. Pull the yarn gently so that it lies around the fingers firmly. Remember to hold it at an even tension so that all stitches are the same size.

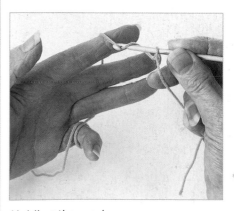

Holding the work.

STARTING OUT

Follow these simple steps to begin crocheting.

1 Hold the hook in the right hand between the thumb and first finger and resting on the second finger, then place the hook under the yarn between the first and second finger on thc lcft hand from front to back.

2 Let the hook catch the yarn and then turn the hook counterclockwise to draw the yarn through the loop on the hook, thus replacing the slip knot with one chain stitch. Repeat this action to make the required number of chains. This is called the foundation or base chain.

CHAIN STITCH (ch)

Besides serving as the foundation of a piece of crochet, chain stitches are also used in patterns to make spaces and arches between stitches or to reach the height of other stitches when turning and working in rows or rounds. To work chain stitch, follow these simple steps.

1 With the yarn in position and the chain loop on the hook, pass the hook under the yarn held in the left hand and catch it with the hook.

2 Turn the hook to draw the yarn through the loop on the hook. Repeat until you have the required number of chains or until the foundation chain is the desired length.

A foundation chain of six stitches (viewed from the front).

A foundation chain of six stitches (viewed from the back).

3 When counting the chain stitches, do not count the original slip loop from which the first chain was made. Count each chain stitch, looking at the front (flatter part) of the chain, ignoring the loop on the hook.

Note Try to work the foundation chain quite loosely. If these stitches are too tight, it will be difficult to work into them, and the edge will be too tight. If the foundation chain does seem too tight, try using a hook one or two sizes larger to achieve a slightly looser chain.

STITCH	ABBREVIATION	TURNING CHAIN
single crochet	sc	1 ch
half double crochet	hdc	2 ch
double crochet	dc	3 ch
triple	tr	4 ch

BASIC STITCHES

A variety of stitches can be worked into the foundation chain to form a crochet fabric. Each stitch gives a different texture and varies in depth. Whatever the stitch, the top edge of each row forms a new line of chains into which the next row is worked.

At the beginning of a row, one or more chain stitches must be worked in order to lift the working loop on the hook to the height of the following stitches; this is called a turning chain. The number of turning-chain stitches needed depends on how many times the yarn is wrapped around the hook to form the first stitch in that row. The guide above gives the number of turning chains needed for the basic stitches.

This is the general rule, but you may find that fewer chains—for example, two turning chains instead of three at the beginning of a row of double crochet—is satisfactory to reach the height of the rest of the stitches and will give a neater edge.

Slip stitch (ss)

This stitch has virtually no depth and is used to work over a fabric made from other stitches. It can be used to move from one point in the fabric to another—for example, to decrease a number of stitches at the armhole shaping, thus avoiding having to break the yarn and rejoin

it. A slip stitch is also used to close a ring when working in rounds and for finishing the garment by joining two pieces together.

To work into a base chain (or stitch), insert the hook into the second chain (or next stitch) from the hook, wind the yarn around the hook—called "yarn over hook" or just "yarn over"—and draw it through both loops on the hook. Repeat this action until the required position is reached. Then continue as stated in the instructions.

Working a slip-stitch row.

Note When working into the base chain, take the hook under two strands of each chain unless otherwise instructed.

Note It is best to count the number of stitches in the row periodically, to check that you still have the required number.

PLACING STITCHES

Most stitches are worked under both strands of the top of a stitch, and this is how to work the stitches in this book unless told otherwise (A).

A different effect is created if only the front or back strand of the stitch is worked into. For example, if you work into the back strand of each stitch on every row, the unworked front loop will give a ridge effect (B).

To create a lacy effect, work into the space between the stitches on the previous row, instead of the two strands at the top of the stitch (C). This will open up the stitches on the previous row. It is quick and easy to do, especially when using textured or bulky yarns, which can be difficult to handle when working into the tops of stitches in the usual way.

Single crochet (sc)

Single crochet creates a dense fabric when used alone. It is popular for working crochet edgings.

Single crochet fabric.

To work single crochet, follow these steps.

1 At the start of a row of sc, begin with 1 chain for turning. Put the hook into the second stitch to the left of the hook. Yarn over hook and draw loop through. There are now 2 loops on the hook.

2 Yarn over hook and draw it through the 2 loops on the hook. Now 1 loop remains on the hook. Continue working each stitch this way.

3 After the last stitch, turn and work 1 chain to count as the first single crochet of the next row, skip the first single crochet of the previous row, then work 1 single crochet into each stitch, including the turning chain at the beginning of the previous row.

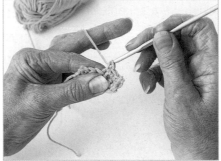

Note In some patterns the turning chain is counted as the first stitch in the row, while in others it is disregarded. Follow the instructions given on the pattern, and be consistent throughout the work.

Half-double crochet (hdc)

This stitch is halfway between a single crochet and a double crochet. It, too, is a popular fabric and not as dense as single crochet.

Half-double crochet fabric.

1 Begin with 2 chains for turning. Wind the yarn over the hook, put the hook into the third stitch to the left of the hook (including turning-chain stitches); yarn over hook and draw a

loop through. There are now 3 loops on the hook.

2 Yarn over hook and draw the yarn through the 3 loops on the hook. Now 1 loop remains on the hook. Work each stitch this way.

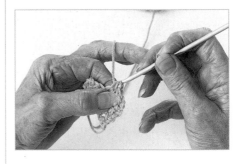

3 After the last stitch, turn and make 2 turning chains, to count as the first half-double crochet, then work one half-double into each stitch to the end of the work, including the turning chain at the beginning of the previous row.

Double crochet (dc)

This is one of the most commonly used stitches, because it is of medium height and produces a light fabric that is firm but also flexible.

Double crochet fabric.

1 Begin with 3 chains for turning. Wind the yarn around the hook, then put the hook into the fourth stitch to the left of the hook (including turning chains), yarn over hook, and draw through a loop. There are now 3 loops on the hook.

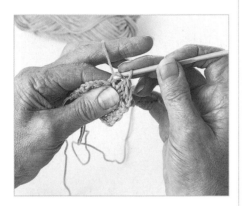

2 Wind the yarn over the hook and draw it through the first 2 loops on the hook. Yarn over hook and draw it through the remaining 2 loops. Now 1 loop remains on the hook. Continue working each stitch this way.

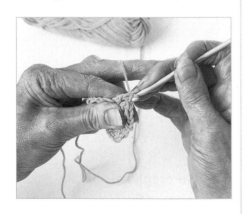

3 After the last stitch, turn and make 3 turning chain, to count as the first double crochet, then work one double crochet into each stitch to the end of the work, including the third of the 3 turning chains at the beginning of the previous row.

Triple crochet (tr)

This stitch is worked in the same way as the double but is taller. It is used mainly for openwork patterns. A fabric made solely of triples would be loose and open, and the rows appear to be joined by "stems."

A scarf worked in triples, using thick yarn and a large crochet hook, would be a suitable project for the beginner.

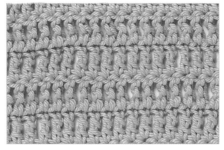

Triple crochet fabric.

1 Start with 4 chains for turning. Wind the yarn around the hook twice, then put the hook into the fifth stitch to the left of the hook (including turning chains); yarn over hook and draw a loop through. There are now 4 loops on the hook.

2 Wind the yarn over the hook and draw through the first 2 loops on the hook (there are now 3 loops on the hook).

3 Wind the yarn over the hook and draw it through the first 2 loops on the hook (there are now 2 loops on the hook).

4 Yarn over hook and draw it through the remaining 2 loops on the hook. Now 1 loop remains on the hook. Continue working each stitch this way.

5 After the last stitch, turn and make 4 turning chains, to count as the first triple, then work one triple into each stitch to the end of the work, including the fourth chain of the 4 turning chains at the beginning of the previous row.

WORKING LONGER STITCHES

Longer stitches—double triple (dtr), triple triple (trtr), quadruple triple (quadtr), and quintuple triple (quintr)—are worked in basically the same way as the double, by wrapping the yarn 3, 4, 5, etc. times around the hook before you start the stitch, and by wrapping and drawing it through 2 loops more times to complete the stitch.

STITCH	ABBREVIATION	TURNING CHAIN	YARN OVER HOOK
Triple	(tr)	4 ch	4 times
Double triple	(dtr)	5 ch	5 times
Triple triple	(trtr)	6 ch	6 times
Quadruple triple	(quadtr or qtr)	7 ch	7 times

FASTENING OFF

Fasten off the working yarn permanently when the last stitch has been made; cut the yarn, leaving a short end of approximately 2 in. (5 cm), or longer if you need to sew pieces together; draw the end through the loop on the hook and tighten it gently.

INCREASING AND DECREASING

Increases and decreases are used to give a garment shape and are worked by adding or taking away a number of stitches to or from a row, such as decreasing for the neckline or increasing for sleeve shaping. Shaping is usually worked at the ends of rows, but it can also be worked during the course of a row.

Single increase

To increase one stitch, simply work twice into the same stitch.

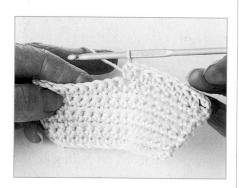

Note When increasing at each end of the row, work twice into the first and last stitches of the previous row. When using thick yarns, it is best to work the increases into the second stitch at the beginning and into the next-to-last stitch at the end of the row. This will give a smoother edge.

If you need to increase more than one stitch at one time, it is better to increase two stitches at regular intervals across a row than to work a larger number of stitches into one space.

Multiple increases

When increasing a number of stitches at both ends of a row—for example, to add sleeves to the main body of a garment—you need to work additional chains at the beginning and end of the row.

1 When you reach the end of the last row before the increases, work a foundation chain instead of a turning chain. Work one chain for each of the new stitches, plus any turning chains.

2 Then turn and work across the row in the usual way.

3 When you reach the end of the row, you again need a length of foundation chain, but you cannot just work the chain from this point, because it would then serve as a foundation for the following row.

Because of the height of crochet stitches, the work would look unbalanced. Instead, remove the hook from the working loop (pulling the loop up a bit so it doesn't unravel); using a separate length or ball of yarn, work the required number of foundation chains (no turning chain is needed) and fasten off. Return to the working loop and continue on the new stitches.

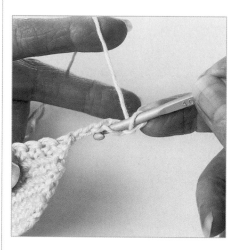

Note Count the stitches to make sure you have the correct number, as stated in the pattern.

Single decrease

To decrease one stitch, simply work two stitches together as one. That is, work the first stitch up to, but not including, the step that would complete the stitch; then work a second stitch into the next stitch in the row below and complete it and the first stitch at the same time.

This basic method can be used to decrease several stitches together. Specific instructions will normally be given in the pattern and abbreviated, for example, dc2tog or tr3tog.

Working two stitches together.

Another method of decreasing within a row is simply to skip a stitch in the previous row.

Decrease one single crochet during the course of a row

To decrease one single crochet in the course of a row, just skip one stitch of the previous row at the stated point; this will not show as a gap, because single crochet is a short stitch.

Decrease one half-double crochet during the course of a row

Work along the row to the stated position.

1 Yarn over hook and insert hook into the next stitch, yarn over hook and draw through loop (3 loops on hook), yarn over hook and insert hook into next stitch, yarn over hook and draw through loop (five loops on hook).

2 Yarn over hook and draw through all loops on hook. One half double has now been decreased.

Decrease one double crochet (and longer stitches) during the course of a row

Work along the row to the stated position and follow these steps.

1 Yarn over hook and insert hook into the next stitch, yarn over hook and draw through loop, yarn over hook and draw through 2 loops on hook.

2 Yarn over hook and insert hook into next stitch, yarn over hook and draw through loop, yarn over hook and draw through 2 loops on hook.

3 Yarn over hook and draw through remaining 3 loops on hook. One double has been decreased.

Longer stitches are worked in the same way, by wrapping and drawing yarn through 2 loops more times, finishing by drawing it through the remaining 3 loops on the hook.

Multiple decrease at beginning of a row

To decrease a number of stitches at the beginning of a row, slip-stitch across the stated number of stitches to be decreased and into

the next stitch, then work the required turning chain (to count as the first stitch) and work in pattern to the end of the row. If stitches need to be decreased at the end of the same row, simply leave those stitches unworked and turn to begin the next row.

Working a multiple decrease.

JOINING A NEW YARN AND CHANGING COLORS

In crochet it is better to avoid tying knots when joining a new yarn. Always try to join a new ball of yarn at the row end to prevent the change from being visible; any long ends can be used to sew up the garment when completed.

Joining yarn at end of a row

When joining a new yarn or changing color, work the last stitch using the old yarn until you reach the final stage (with 2 loops on the hook). Leave the old yarn at the back of the work and pick up the new yarn. Draw the new yarn through to complete the stitch.

Joining yarn at the end of a row.

Joining yarn mid-row

If you need to change to a new color in the middle of a row, follow these steps.

1 Work the last stitch using the old color until you reach the final stage (with 2 loops on the hook).

2 Complete the stitch with the new color. Lay the ends of yarn together over the previous row, and work the next 4 or 5 stitches enclosing the ends. Trim the ends. This technique avoids having to sew in all the ends after the work is completed.

However, if you are working a loose or lacy stitch pattern, it is better to leave the loose ends at the back of the work and weave them in after the crochet is completed. This prevents the changeover from being visible on the right side of the work.

When working in narrow horizontal stripes, work the last stitch on the previous row with the old yarn until the final stage is reached (with 2 loops on the hook), and complete the stitch with the new yarn so that your new color is already in place for the new row. The yarn not in use can be carried up the side of the work until needed again. With deeper or irregular horizontal stripes, it is best to cut the yarn and rejoin, following the instructions given above.

STITCH GROUPS

Most crochet stitch patterns are worked using the basic stitches. Varied effects can be achieved by inserting the hook into the fabric in a different way or a different number of times. Among the decorative stitches that can be produced are picots, shells, crab stitch, clusters, bobbles, popcorns, puffs, and relief stitches. Most of these effects are based on stitches as tall as a double crochet and upward. They vary from pattern to pattern, so a special abbreviation is usually given at the beginning of the instructions.

Shells

Stitches can be grouped together—that is, worked into the same place—either as a way of increasing or for a decorative effect. When several complete stitches are grouped in this way at the bottom but not at the top, they form a "fan" or "shell." Different lengths of stitch can be used to make shells.

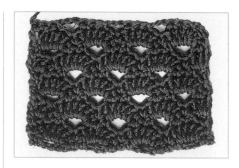

Example of shell stitch.

Shell stitch used as an edging.

Picot stitch

A picot is made from 3, 4, or 5 chain stitches (according to the size of picot desired), which are formed into a tiny loop either by working a slip stitch into the first chain of the picot or by working a single crochet into the same place where the picot began. Follow the pattern instructions as to which method should be used.

Example of picot stitch.

Clusters

A cluster also consists of a combination of stitches, but in this case, the base of each stitch is worked into a different stitch; the last loop of each stitch is left on the hook, then the loops are joined at the top by working them together. This method can also be a way of decreasing.

Example of a cluster.

Bobbles

These are ideal for trimmings and edgings on garments. A bobble is made by working a number of stitches (usually 3, 4, or 5) into the same place and leaving the last loop of each stitch on the hook, then working the loops together at the end. Sometimes a chain stitch is used to close the bobble; this will be indicated in the pattern instructions.

Example of a bobble.

Popcorn stitch

This is more pronounced than the cluster or bobble and can be used in Aran-style garments, in edgings, or in all-over raised decorative patterns. It consists of a group of complete stitches, usually worked into the same place.

Work the required number of stitches given in the pattern, then take the hook out of the working loop and into the top of the first stitch at the beginning of the group of stitches. Then draw the working loop through the top of the first stitch, thus bringing together the first and last stitches. Sometimes an extra chain stitch is worked to close the popcorn firmly. This will be indicated in the pattern instructions.

If a popcorn is worked on the wrong side of the fabric, make sure that the stitches are pushed through to the right side so that the popcorn shows on that side of the work.

Example of popcorn stitches.

Crab stitch

This stitch is often used as a final edging stitch and produces a corded effect. It is basically single crochet but worked backward—preferably after a right-side row.

After completing the right-side row, do not turn the work; instead, insert the hook back into the last stitch just worked, pull the yarn through the stitch from back to front, then complete the single crochet by drawing a loop through the 2 loops on the hook in the usual way. Work another single crochet into the next stitch to the right, and so on, to the end. Sometimes this stitch can produce a rippled effect. If this happens, just skip the occasional stitch on the previous row or use a smaller crochet hook for the crab stitch.

Crab stitch used as an edging.

RELIEF STITCHES

These stitches are worked around the stem, or "post," of a stitch on one or more rows below the row in progress. If relief stitches are worked into a row 2 or more rows below, longer stitches, such as triples or double triples, will need to be used. The technique creates a heavily textured fabric that is reversible. It is therefore good for ribbing (although this does not create an elastic fabric, as in knitting) and is suitable for heavier, outer garments or blankets and rugs.

Example of relief stitches.

Raised double on front

To work a raised double at the front of the fabric (dc/rf): Yarn over hook, then insert the hook from right to left under the stem of the stitch below; complete the stitch in the usual way.

Working at the front of the fabric.

Raised double on back

To work a raised double at the back of the fabric (dc/rb): Yarn over hook, then take the hook behind the work and insert it from right to left under the stem of the stitch below; complete the stitch in the usual way.

Working at the back of the fabric.

WORKING ROUND AND SQUARE MOTIFS

All motifs worked from the center outward can develop into various shapes and forms, including circles, squares, flowers, snowflakes, hexagons, octagons, and triangles.

There is usually no need to turn the work at the end of a row, but it will be necessary to work the required turning chain to achieve the height for the next round.

1 Begin by making the number of chains specified in the pattern, and join them in a ring with a slip stitch into the first chain.

Joining the chain into a ring.

2 The first round is worked into the ring itself (not into the individual stitches). The round is completed by working a slip stitch into the first stitch of the round. In the illustration, the first round is made of triple stitches.

Working the first round.

3 Sometimes the stitches of the first round are worked into a slip loop; this is used when no hole is to be left in the center of the motif. When the round is complete, pull the slip loop gently to close the hole.

4 When the last stitch has been made, fasten off in the usual way. If the motifs are to be sewn together afterward, it is advisable to leave extra yarn or thread at the end of the motif and use this to sew the motifs together.

Fastening off.

JOINING MOTIFS

Motifs can be joined, either after they are completed or on the last round to be worked.

If the motifs are to be joined as they are being made, instructions on how to do this are usually given in the pattern. When joining motifs after they are completed, first press and block them, if necessary, so that they are all the same size. Weave in any ends, then lay the motifs out in the desired arrangement. Using the same yarn, work overcasting stitches into the corresponding back loops along the edges of two adjacent motifs. Or for a stronger seam, work into both loops of the edge stitches. Either method produces a flat seam. Join all the motifs in a row, then join the rows using the same method.

FOLLOWING A CHART

Sometimes it is necessary to include a stitch diagram with a pattern, as in the case of a complex lacy design. Stitch diagrams are often given as a visual aid, showing the right side uppermost, to clarify a written set of instructions. It is easier to follow a chart than to read a lengthy written pattern. On the diagram a symbol is used to replace each type of stitch. Each stitch diagram will have a key. Before using a crochet chart, you need to familiarize yourself with the symbols. The basic symbols are listed below and are used internationally.

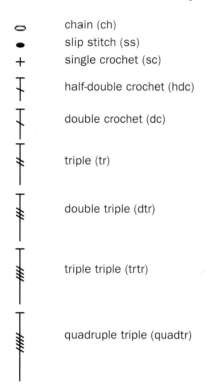

⌒	chain (ch)
●	slip stitch (ss)
+	single crochet (sc)
Ŧ	half-double crochet (hdc)
⊤	double crochet (dc)
⊤	triple (tr)
⊤	double triple (dtr)
⊤	triple triple (trtr)
⊤	quadruple triple (quadtr)

Note From the double onward, the diagonal lines crossing the t-bar represent the number of times the yarn has to be wrapped around the hook to produce the stitch. For example, the double triple has 3 diagonal lines, meaning that the yarn has to be wrapped around the hook 3 times.

EDGINGS

Crocheted edgings can be used to decorate household items such as place mats, tablecloths and napkins, towels and bed linens. They are also used on crocheted items to give a more finished look to a completed garment on cuffs, collars, hem edges, or pockets, and to help hold the main sections in place to prevent any stretching. Edging designs range from plain to fancy lace patterns. As a decoration for linens, they are made separately and sewn on, but for crocheted items they are normally worked directly onto the item. They can be worked in rows or rounds and are usually worked on a foundation row of single crochet in order to give a firmer edge.

Working top and bottom edges

Edgings are usually worked using a smaller hook than that used for the main pieces in order to give a firmer edge, which won't stretch.

Begin by working with the right side of the garment facing, usually at one end of a seam. Working an edge onto the top of a row is quite simple: Just work the edging stitches as if you were working another row of the main fabric. When working onto a hem edge (foundation row), work into the loops of chain stitches left unworked during the first row (see Note under "Slip stitch," page 15).

Working edging along the top of a row.

Working row ends and curved edges

Working along the row ends is a little more difficult. It is best to try to work stitches so that they are evenly spaced but slit properly to hold the edge in slightly. Too few stitches will pull the work in too much, and too many will cause the edge to splay out. There is no rule. Try out the edge stitch on your gauge swatch before working the real thing to try to estimate correctly the number of stitches you will need to work into the row ends.

Space the stitches evenly along the row ends to give a flat and smooth appearance.

Working edging along row ends.

On an inner curved edge, as on a neck edge, you would have to work fewer stitches into the row ends than on the front edge of a garment to obtain a smooth line.

Working edging along an inner curve.

On an outer curved edge, as on a corner, you would have to increase into the corner stitch for a smooth line. As a general guide, 3 stitches are usually worked into each corner stitch.

Separate edgings

Separate edgings can be worked in one length and then sewn onto a ready-made item or a separate crochet item afterward.

Before beginning a separate edging, calculate the finished length, allowing extra for any curved edges. In the case of a circular mat or cloth, allow enough so that the edging can be eased in when sewn in place to lie flat. Some patterned edgings curve automatically and are suitable for collars. If sewn to a straight edge—for example, on a V-neck or on the front edges of a wraparound cardigan—this type of deliberately curved edging will fall as a ruffle.

It is best to sew on a separate edging by hand rather than by machine. Place the item and edging together with the right sides facing and edges matching. Using a matching yarn or thread, slip-stitch or overcast the edging to the item, taking care not to pull the thread too tightly. If there are any corners, gather the crochet slightly so that the edge will lie flat.

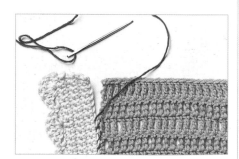

Attaching a separate edging.

MAKING BUTTONHOLES

Buttonholes can be worked either vertically or horizontally.

To work a vertical buttonhole, work up to the point where the buttonhole is to be made, then turn and work on these stitches until the desired depth of the buttonhole is reached. Next, return to the other side of the buttonhole and work the same number of rows. Then continue working across all the stitches.

Making a vertical buttonhole.

To work a horizontal buttonhole—for example, in single crochet—just skip 2 (or more) stitches and work the equivalent number of chains. On the return row, work the same number of single crochets over the chain stitches on the previous row.

Making a horizontal buttonhole.

FINISHING GARMENTS

Even the simplest garments require careful finishing. It is worth spending time doing this in order to produce a professional finish.

Begin by weaving in any loose ends. Refer to the manufacturer's instructions on the yarn label for pressing and care instructions. Some yarns will be ruined if a steam iron is used for pressing. For synthetic yarns, cover each piece of the garment with a damp cloth and leave this to dry. Natural fibers can be covered with a damp cloth and pressed gently with a steam iron.

JOINING SEAMS

Use a large tapestry needle or yarn needle, both of which have blunt points, for sewing the garment together. Normally, the same yarn used for the crochet should be used for sewing; however, if the crochet uses a thick or highly textured yarn, it is best to use a thinner, smooth yarn in a matching color.

Sewn edge seam

To join with a sewn edge seam, place the pieces edge to edge with the wrong sides uppermost and slip-stitch through one loop of each piece. If a firmer seam is required—for example, at the shoulders—join the pieces with backstitch.

Sewn edge seam.

Crocheted seam

The most flexible way of joining two pieces of crochet together is by working a crocheted seam. Place the right sides together and work a row of single crochet—or slip stitch, if preferred—along the edges, working under two loops of each edge.

Crocheted seam.

Decorative seam

If a decorative edge is required, place the pieces together with wrong sides facing and join with single crochet, working under two loops of each edge. Pieces can also be joined, right sides uppermost, using a fancy openwork stitch.

Decorative seam.

ZIPPERS

Always insert an open-ended zipper with the fastener closed to ensure that both sides match.

Pin the zipper in position, taking care not to stretch the crochet. Use an ordinary sewing needle and matching thread. With the right side of the work facing, sew in the zipper with backstitch, keeping as close to the crocheted edge as possible.

Always work from top to bottom and take care not to cover the zipper teeth. Sew down the zipper edges on the inside afterward.

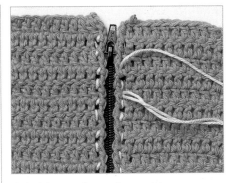

Stitching a zipper in position.

SEWN-ON POCKETS

Sew a pocket in place with slip stitch, taking care to keep the lines of the pocket and main fabric straight. A useful tip is first to use a fine knitting needle, pointed at both ends, to pick up every alternate stitch along the line of the main fabric, then to alternately catch one stitch from the edge of the pocket and one stitch from the needle. Make sure that the lower edge of the pocket lies in a straight line across a row of the main fabric.

Sewing a pocket in place.

TASSELS

Cut a piece of cardboard the same length that you want the tassel to be. Wind yarn around the cardboard to the required thickness and cut. Thread a needle with yarn and pull it under the strands at the top of the card. Tie securely, leaving a long end. Cut through the yarn at the other end of the card. Wind the long end of yarn around the tassel about ⅝ in. (1.5 cm) from the top and secure it by pushing the needle through the middle of the tassel. Trim evenly.

Making tassels.

FRINGE

Cut the yarn into pieces just over twice the desired finished length of the fringe. Fold each group of strands in half and, with the wrong side of the fabric facing you, draw a loop through the edge stitch using a crochet hook. Then draw the loose ends of the strands through this loop and pull down tightly to form a knot. Repeat at regular intervals.

Making fringe.

SWEATERS AND TOPS

In this chapter you will find a beautiful selection of sweaters and tops, ranging from casual jackets and wraparound tops to delicate lacy tunics, sizzling sleeveless tops, and a pretty tie-front bolero. Many of the garments can be worn with jeans or dressed up for special occasions. The wide range of colors, stitch patterns, and styles means that there is something here to suit everyone.

Asymmetrical Jacket

This stylish garment is quick and easy to work, using a large crochet hook and simple double crochet. The interesting yarn creates a fascinating fabric, while the button bands are worked in a finer yarn. Just the thing for cool fall days.

Skill level: BEGINNER

MEASUREMENTS

To fit bust

32–34	36–38	40–42	in.
81–86	91–97	102–107	cm

Actual width

37½	40	45	in.
95	102	115	cm

Length from shoulder

24	25	26½	in.
61	63	67	cm

Sleeve seam

18	18	18½	in.
46	46	47	cm

MATERIALS

- 14 (15:16) × 50 g (1¾ oz.) balls of Sirdar Tuscany in Gypsy 665 (A)
- 1 × 50 g (1¾ oz.) ball of Sirdar Country Style DK in Heather 529 (B)
- G/6 (4.25 mm) and L/11 (8 mm) crochet hook
- 8 buttons, ¾ in. (2 cm) in diameter

GAUGE

8 sts and 6 rows to 4 in. (10 cm) measured over pattern using L/11 (8 mm) crochet hook. Change hook size, if necessary, to obtain this gauge.

ABBREVIATIONS

dc2tog—leaving last loop of each on hook, work 1 dc into each of next 2 sts, yoh and draw through all 3 loops to dec 1 st.
See also page 11.

NOTE
Figures in parentheses refer to the larger sizes; where only one set of figures is given, this refers to all sizes.

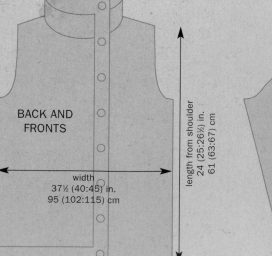

BACK AND FRONTS

width
37½ (40:45) in.
95 (102:115) cm

length from shoulder
24 (25:26½) in.
61 (63:67) cm

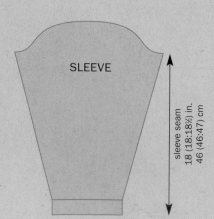

SLEEVE

sleeve seam
18 (18:18½) in.
46 (46:47) cm

JACKET

BACK

Using larger hook and A, ch 40 (43:48) loosely.

Row 1 (RS) Skip 3 ch (counts as 1 dc), 1 dc into next and each ch to end, turn. 38 (41:46) sts.

Row 2 (WS) Ch 3 (counts as 1 dc), skip first dc, * 1 dc into sp before next dc and below all horizontal threads connecting sts; rep from * to end, but do not work 1 dc into sp before the 3 turning ch, work 1 dc into top of 3 ch, turn. 38 (41:46) sts.

Row 2 forms patt.

Patt until work measures 15¼ (15¼ :16) in. (39 [39:41] cm) from beg, ending with a WS row.

Shape armholes

Next row Ss across and into the 4th (4th:5th) st, ch 3 for first dc, patt to last 3 (3:4) sts, turn. 32 (35:38) sts.

Next 2 rows Ch 3 (counts as 1 dc), dc2tog, patt to last 3 sts, dc2tog, 1 dc in top of 3 ch. 28 (31:34) sts.

Patt straight until armholes measure 7½ (8¼:9) in. (19 [21:23] cm) from beg of shaping, ending with a WS row.

Shape shoulders

Next row Ss across and into the 5th (5th:6th) st, patt to the last 4 (4:5) sts, turn.

Next row Ss across and into the 5th (6th:6th) st, patt to last 4 (5:5) sts.

Fasten off. 12 (13:14) sts.

RIGHT FRONT

Using larger hook and A, ch 27 (29:32).

Row 1 (RS) Skip 3 ch (counts as 1 dc), 1 dc into next and each ch to end, turn. 25 (27:30) sts.

Cont in patt as Back until work measures 15¼ (15¼:16) in. (39 [39:41] cm) from beg, ending with a WS row.

Shape armhole

Next row Patt to last 3 (3:4) sts, turn. 22 (24:26) sts.

Next row 3 ch (counts as 1 dc), dc2tog, patt to end.

Next row Patt to last 3 sts, dc2tog, 1 dc in top of 3 ch, turn. 20 (22:24) sts.

Patt straight until armhole measures 6 rows shorter than Back to beg of shoulder, ending with a WS row.

Shape neck

Next row Ss across and into the 11th (12th:13th) st, patt to end, turn.

Next row Patt to last 3 sts, dc2tog, 1 dc in top of 3 ch.

Next row 3 ch (counts as 1 dc), dc2tog, patt to end. 8 (9:10) sts.

Patt 3 rows straight, ending with a WS row.

Shape shoulder

Next row Patt to last 4 (4:5) sts. Fasten off.

LEFT FRONT

Using larger hook and A, ch 15 (16:18).

Row 1 Ch 3 (counts as 1 dc), 1 dc into next and each ch to end, turn. 13 (14:16) sts.

Cont in patt as Back until work measures 15¼ (15¼:16) in. (39 [39:41] cm) from beg, ending with a WS row.

Shape armhole

Next row Ss across and into the 4th (4th:5th) st, ch 3 for first dc, patt to end, turn. 10 (11:12) sts.

Next row Patt to last 3 sts, dc2tog, 1 dc in top of 3 ch.

Next row 3 ch (counts as 1 dc), dc2tog, patt to end. 8 (9:10) sts.

Cont straight until armhole measures 4 rows shorter than Back to beg of shoulder, ending with a WS row. Place a marker at neck edge. Patt 4 rows, ending with a WS row.

Shape shoulder

Next row Ss across and into the 5th (5th:6th) st, patt to end. Fasten off.

SLEEVES (make 2)

Using larger hook and A, ch 21 (23:24).

Row 1 (RS) Skip 3 ch (counts as 1 dc), 1 dc into next and each ch to end, turn. 19 (21:22) sts.

Cont in patt as Back.

Next inc row Ch 3 (counts as 1 dc), 1 dc into base of 3 ch, patt to last st, 2 dc in last st. Inc 1 st at each end of the 4 (4:5) foll 5th (5th:4th) rows. 29 (31:34) sts.

Patt straight until sleeve measures 17 (17:17¼) in. (43 [43:44] cm) from beg.

Shape top

Next row Ss across and into the 4th (4th:5th) st, patt to the last 3 (3:4) sts, turn. 23 (25:26) sts.
Next row 3 ch (counts as 1 dc) dc2tog, patt to last 3 sts, dc2tog, 1 dc in top of 3 ch, turn.

Rep last row 5 times more, 11 (13:14) sts. Fasten off.

COLLAR

Join shoulders.

With RS facing, using larger hook and A, work 15 (16:17) sc evenly along right front neck edge to shoulder, 12 (13:14) sc across back neck, and 5 sc along Left Front neck edge to marker. 32 (34:36) sts.

Patt 5 rows as for Back. Fasten off.

FINISHING

Set in sleeves. Join side and sleeve seams. Weave in all yarn ends.

Lower edging

Using smaller hook, join B to lower corner of Left Front, ch 1, work 1 row in sc evenly along lower edge of entire jacket, turn. Work 6 more rows in sc. Fasten off.

Cuffs

Using smaller hook, join B at sleeve seam, ch 1, work 1 row in sc evenly along cuff edge, ss to 1 ch, turn.
Next 6 rounds Ch 1, 1 sc in each sc to end, ss to 1 ch, turn. Fasten off. Repeat for second sleeve cuff.

Collar edging

Using smaller hook, join B to RS of collar, ch 1, work 1 row in sc evenly along last row worked for collar, turn. Work 6 more rows in sc. Fasten off.

Button band

Using smaller hook, join B to last row of collar edging, ch 1, work 1 row in sc evenly along edge of collar and left front, turn. Work 6 more rows in sc. Fasten off.

Mark the positions of 8 buttons, the first ¾ in. (2 cm) up from lower edge, the last ¾ in. (2 cm) down from top of collar, and the rest spaced evenly between.

The jacket buttons right up to the collar.

Buttonhole band

Using smaller hook, join B to lower corner of right front, ch 1, work 1 row in sc evenly along right front and collar (same no. of sts as for left front), turn. Work 3 more rows in sc.
Buttonhole row Ch 1, 1 sc in each sc to end, making buttonholes to correspond with markers on left front by working ch 2, then skipping next 2 sc.
Next row Ch 1, 1 sc in each sc to end, working 2 sc into each 2-ch sp for buttonholes.

Work 1 more row in sc. Fasten off.

Sew on buttons to correspond with buttonholes.

Weave in all yarn ends.

Cool-Weather Capelet

The texture of this simple pattern is defined with crossed stitches. It is worked in one piece, so there are no seams to sew! The turtleneck makes this capelet warm and comfortable, while an attractive trim on the lower edge adds visual interest.

Skill level: INTERMEDIATE

MEASUREMENTS

To fit bust

32–34	36–38	40–42	in.
81–86	91–97	102–107	cm

Width around hem edge

49	53½	58	in.
124	136	147	cm

Length from top of turtleneck
17½ in. (44 cm)

MATERIALS

• 3 (4:5) × 140 g (5 oz.) balls of Lion Cotton in Rose 140

• G/6 (4.25 mm) crochet hook

GAUGE

14 dc and 7½ rows to 4 in. (10 cm) measured over pattern, using G/6 (4.25 mm) crochet hook. Change hook size, if necessary, to obtain this gauge.

ABBREVIATIONS

dc2tog—leaving last loop of each st on hook, work 1 dc into each of the next 2 sts, yoh and draw through all 3 loops on hook to dec 1 st.
bobble—leaving last loop of each st on hook, work 4 dc into next st, yoh and draw through all 5 loops. *See also page 11.*

NOTE
Figures in parentheses refer to the larger sizes; where only one set of figures is given, this refers to all sizes.

CAPELET

Ch 174 (190:206), ss to first ch to form a ring, taking care not to twist ch.
Foundation round Ch 3 (counts as 1dc), *1 dc in each ch to end, ss to top of 3 ch. 174 (190:206) sts.
Round 1 Ch 4 (counts as 1 dc and 1 ch), skip next st, *1 dc into next st, ch 1, skip next st; rep from * ending ss to 3rd of 4 ch.
Round 2 Ss into first ch sp, ch 4 (counts as 1 tr), taking hook behind 4 ch work 1 tr into ch sp to right of last ch sp worked into, * 1 tr into next free ch sp, taking hook behind last tr work 1 tr into ch sp to right of sp where last tr was worked—pair of crossed tr worked, rep from * to end, ss to top of 4 ch. 87 (95:103) pairs of crossed tr.
Round 3 Ch 3 (counts as 1 dc), 1 dc into each st, ss to top of 3 ch.

These 3 rounds form patt. Patt 8 more rounds, thus ending with a Round 2.
Dec round 1 Ch 3 (counts as 1 dc), 1 dc into each of next 3 (8:6) sts, [dc2tog, 1 dc into each of next 9 (8:8) sts] 15 (17:19) times, dc2tog, 1 dc into each of last 3 (9:7) sts, ss to top of 3 ch. 158 (172:186) sts.

Patt 2 rounds.
Dec round 2 Ch 3 (counts as 1 dc), 1 dc into each of next 2 (3:4) sts, [dc2tog, 1 dc into each of next 4 sts] 25 (27:29) times, dc2tog, 1 dc into each of last 3 (4:5) sts, ss to top of 3 ch. 132 (144:156) sts.

Patt 2 rounds.

Dec round 3 Ch 3 (counts as 1 dc), 1 dc into each of next 2 (3:4) sts, [dc2tog, 1 dc into each of next 3 sts] 25 (27:29) times, dc2tog, 1 dc into each of last 2 (3:4) sts, ss to top of 3 ch. 106 (116:126) sts.

Patt 2 rounds.

Dec round 4 Ch 3 (counts as 1 dc), 1 dc into each of next 1 (2:3) sts, [dc2tog, 1 dc into each of next 2 sts] 25 (27:29) times, dc2tog, 1 dc into each of last 2 (3:4) sts, ss to top of 3 ch. 80 (88:96) sts.

Patt 2 rounds.

Dec round 5 Ch 3 (counts as 1dc), 1 dc into each of next 1 (2:3) sts, [dc2tog, 1 dc into next dc] 25 (27:29) times, dc2tog, 1 dc into each of last 1 (2:3) sts, ss to top of 3 ch. 54 (60:66) sts.

Patt another 6 rounds for turtleneck. Fasten off. Weave in yarn ends.

LOWER EDGE

With RS facing, join yarn at beg of first round.

Round 1 Ch 1 (counts as 1 sc), work in sc evenly around lower edge working into sps between dc and working a multiple of 5 sts, ss to 1 ch, turn.

Round 2 Ch 1 (counts as 1 sc), * ch 5, skip 4 sc, 1 sc into next sc; rep from * ending last rep with ss to 1 ch, turn.

Round 3 Ch 3 (counts as first dc of bobble), leaving last loop of each dc on hook, work 3 dc into same place as ss, yoh and draw through all 4 loops, * ch 3, 1 sc into next 5-ch arch, ch 3, 1 bobble into next sc; rep from * ending ss to top of first bobble.

Round 4 Ch 1 (counts as 1 sc), * 3 sc into 3-ch arch, 1sc into sc, 3 sc into 3-ch arch, 1 sc in bobble; rep from * ending ss to 1 ch. Fasten off. Weave in yarn ends.

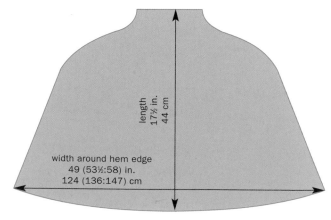

length 17½ in. 44 cm

width around hem edge
49 (53½:58) in.
124 (136:147) cm

The versatile design makes it easy to wear with pants or a skirt.

Summer Breezes

Quick and easy to crochet, this sleeveless top is the perfect project for a beginner. It is made using a soft cotton yarn. A matching belt in the same stitch pattern (see page 37) is the perfect finishing touch.

Skill level: INTERMEDIATE

MEASUREMENTS

To fit bust

32	34	36	38	in.
81	86	91	97	cm

Actual width

35½	38	41	43	in.
90	96	104	109	cm

Length from shoulder

21	21¼	21¾	22	in.
53	54	55	56	cm

MATERIALS

- 3 (4:4:4) × 100 g (3½ oz.) balls of Sirdar Breeze DK in Buttermilk 063

- E/4 (3.50 mm) and G/6 (4.25 mm) crochet hooks

GAUGE

15 dc and 10 rows to 4 in. (10 cm) measured over double crochet pattern, using G/6 (4.25 mm) crochet hook. Change hook size, if necessary, to obtain this gauge.

ABBREVIATIONS

dc2tog—leaving last loop of each st on hook, work 1 dc into each of the next 2sts, yoh and draw through rem 3 loops, so dec 1 st. *See also page 11.*

NOTE

Figures in parentheses refer to the larger sizes; where only one set of figures is given, this refers to all sizes.

TOP

BACK

Using larger hook, ch 70 (74:80:84).

Foundation row (RS) 2 dc into 4th ch from hook, *skip 1 ch, 2 dc into next ch—pair of dc worked; rep from * to last 2 ch, skip 1 ch, 1 dc into last ch, turn. 33 (35:38:40) pairs of dc plus 1 st at each end.

Patt row Ch 3, skip first dc, * 2 dc into sp at center of next pair of dc, rep from * to end, 1 dc into top of 3 ch, turn. This row forms patt.

Patt 1 more row.

Shape sides

** **Dec row** Ch 3 (counts as 1 dc), dc2tog, patt to last 3 sts, dc2tog, 1 dc into top of 3 ch, turn. Patt 3 rows **. Rep from ** to ** once, then work dec row again. 62 (66:72:76) sts.

Patt 5 rows.

Inc and take into patt 1 st at each end of next row, then on 2 foll 6th rows. 68 (72:78:82) sts.

Cont straight until work measures 13½ in. (34 cm) from beg, ending with a WS row.

Shape armholes

Next row Ss across and into the 5th (5th:6th:6th) st, ch 3 (counts as 1 dc), patt to last 4 (4:5:5) sts, turn. 60 (64:68:72) sts. ***

Dec 1 st at each end of next 6 (6:7:7) rows. 48 (52:54:58) sts.

Cont straight until armholes measure 6 (6¼:6½:7) in. (15 [16:17:18] cm) from beg.

Shape back neck

Next row Ch 3 (counts as 1 dc), patt 8 (9:10:11), turn. Work on these 9 (10:11:12) sts for first side.

Work 2 rows. Fasten off.

Return to rem sts. Leave the center 30 (32:32:34) sts, rejoin yarn to next st, ch 3 (counts as 1 dc), patt to end. 9 (10:11:12) sts.

Work 2 rows. Fasten off.

FRONT

Work as given for Back to ***.

Dec 1 st at each end of next 3 rows.

54 (58:62:66) sts.

Shape neck

Next row Ch 3, dc2tog, patt 12 (13:15:16) sts, turn. Work on these 14 (15:17:18) sts for first side.

Dec 1 st at each end of next 2 (2:3:3) rows. 10 (11:11:12) sts.

1st and 2nd sizes only

Dec 1 st at neck edge on next row. 9 (10:11:12) sts.

All sizes

Patt straight until Front measures the same as Back to shoulder. Fasten off.

With RS facing, skip the center 24 (26:26:28) sts, rejoin yarn to next st, ch 3 (counts as 1 dc), patt to last 3 sts, dc2tog, 1 dc in top of 3 ch, turn.

Complete this side to match the first side.

FINISHING

Join shoulders and side seams. Weave in yarn ends.

Neck edging

With RS facing and using smaller hook, join yarn at one shoulder seam, ch 1 (counts as 1 sc), work a row of sc evenly around neck edge, ss to 1 ch, turn.

Next row Ch 1 (counts as 1 sc), 1 sc into each sc to end, ss to 1 ch.

Work 1 more row in sc. Fasten off.

Armbands

With RS facing and using smaller hook, join yarn to one side seam at underarm and work as given for neck edging.

Lower edge

With RS facing and using smaller hook, join yarn to seam at lower edge and work as given for neck edging.

Belt

Using smaller hook, ch 6.

Patt as given for Back for desired length.

Edging

Ch 1 (counts as 1 sc), 1 sc into corner, work in sc along all edges, working 2 sc into each corner, ss to 1 ch. Fasten off. Weave in all yarn ends.

Cords (make 2)

Using larger hook, ch 130.

Next row 1 sc into 2nd ch from hook, 1 sc into each ch to end. Fasten off. Repeat.

Fold each cord in half, pass looped end through center of one end of belt, pass ends of cord through loop.

This top can be worn with jeans or with a skirt for a dressier occasion.

length 21 (21½:21½:22)in. 53 (54:55:56) cm

width 35½ (38:41:43) in. 90 (96:104:109) cm

BACK AND FRONT

Casual Cardigan

This long-line cardigan in a lightweight silky looking yarn is made from a mesh pattern of blocks and spaces, with a fancy edging on the cuffs and lower hem. Perfect to wear over jeans or even with a casual dress for evening.

★★★
Skill level: ADVANCED

MEASUREMENTS

To fit bust

32–34	36–38	40–42	in.
81–87	91–97	102–107	cm

Actual width around bust

35	40	44½	in.
89	101	113	cm

Length from shoulder (including border)

40	41	41½	in.
102	104	106	cm

Sleeve seam (including cuff)

21 in. (53 cm)

MATERIALS

- 15 (16:17) × 50 g (1¾ oz.) balls of Sirdar Silky Look DK in Stone 905

- G/6 (4.25 mm) crochet hook

GAUGE

20 sts and 9 rows to 4 in. (10 cm) measured over double crochet using G/6 (4.25 mm) mm crochet hook. Change hook size, if necessary, to obtain this gauge.

ABBREVIATIONS

bobble—leaving last loop of each dtr on hook, work 3 dtr into next st, yoh and draw through all 4 loops.

cluster—leaving last loop of each dc on hook, work 3 dc into next st or sp, yoh and draw through all 4 loops.

dc2(3)tog—leaving last loop of each dc on hook, work 1 dc into each of next 2 (3) sts, yoh and draw through all 3 (4) loops, so dec 1 (2) sts. *See also page 11.*

NOTES

Figures in parentheses refer to the larger sizes; where only one set of figures is given, this refers to all sizes.
When dec over filet patt (1 dc, ch 1, skip next st, 1 dc in next st), work a dc into ch sp to work dc3tog.
When dec over cluster patt [ch 1 (2), skip cluster, 1 cluster in next 2-ch sp] work 1 (2) dc into 1 (2) ch sp to work dc2(3)tog.

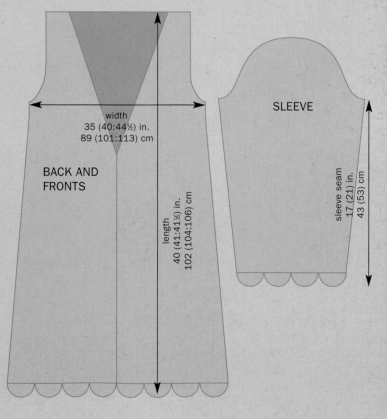

width
35 (40:44½) in.
89 (101:113) cm

BACK AND FRONTS

length
40 (41:41½) in.
102 (104:106) cm

SLEEVE

sleeve seam
17 (21) in.
43 (53) cm

CARDIGAN

BACK

Ch 119 (131:143).

Row 1 (RS) 1 dc into 4th ch from hook, 1dc into each ch to end, turn. 117 (129:141) sts.

Row 2 Ch 4 (counts as 1 dc and 1 ch), skip first 2 dc, *1 dc into next dc, ch 1, skip next dc, rep from * to end, 1 dc into top of 3 ch, turn. 58 (64:70) squares.

Rows 3, 4, and 5 Ch 4 (counts as 1 dc and 1 ch), skip first dc and ch, *1 dc into next dc, ch 1, skip next ch; rep from * to end, 1 dc in 3rd of 4 ch, turn.

Row 6 Ch 3 (counts as 1 dc), skip first dc, *1 dc into next ch sp, 1 dc into next dc; rep from * to end, working last dc into 3rd of 4 ch, turn. 117 (129:141) sts.

Row 7 Ch 5 (counts as 1 dc and 2 ch), skip first 3 dc; *1 cluster into next dc, ch 2, skip 2 dc; rep from * to last 3 dc, 1 cluster into next dc, ch 1, skip next st, 1 dc into top of 3 ch, turn. 38 (42:46) clusters.

Row 8 Ch 3 (counts as 1 dc), 1 cluster into first 1-ch sp, *ch 2, 1 cluster in next 2-ch sp; rep from * ending ch 2, 1 cluster into last sp, 1 dc in 3rd of 5 ch, turn. 39 (43:47) clusters.

Row 9 Ch 5, * 1 cluster into next 2-ch sp, ch 2, rep from * ending 1 cluster into last 2-ch sp, ch 1, skip next st, 1 dc into top of 3 ch, turn.

Row 10 Ch 3 (counts as 1 dc), 1 dc into next 1-ch sp, 1 dc into top of next cluster, * 2 dc into next 2-ch sp, 1 dc into top of next cluster; rep from * ending 2 dc in last sp, 1 dc into 3rd of 5 ch, turn. 117 (129:141) sts.
Rows 2–10 form patt.

Patt 18 more rows.

Shape sides

Row 29 Dc3tog, patt to last 3 sts, dc3tog, turn. 113 (125:137) sts.

Patt 7 more rows.

Row 37 Dc3tog, patt to last 3 sts, dc3tog, turn. 109 (121:133) sts.

Patt 5 more rows.

Row 43 Dc3tog, patt to last 3 sts, dc3tog, turn. 105 (117:129) sts.

Patt 5 more rows.

Cont to dec in this way on the next and 3 foll 4th rows. 89 (101:113) sts.

Work 9 more patt rows straight, ending with a 7th patt row.

Shape armholes

Next row Ss across and into the 10th (11th:12th) st, patt to last 9 (10:11) sts, turn. 71 (81:91) sts.

Dc2tog at each end of next 4 rows. 63 (73:83) sts. Patt another 12 (14:16) rows. Fasten off.

LEFT AND RIGHT FRONTS
(both alike—patt is reversible)

Ch 61 (67:73).

Row 1 (RS) 1 dc into 4th ch from hook, 1dc into each ch to end, turn. 59 (65:71) sts.

Cont in patt as follows.

Rows 2–6 As given for Back.

Row 7 Ch 5 (counts as 1 dc and 2 ch), skip first 3 dc; *1 cluster into next dc, ch 2, skip 2 dc; rep from * ending, 1 cluster into next dc, 1 dc into top of 3 ch, turn. 19 (21:23) clusters.

Row 8 Ch 4 (counts as 1 dc and 1 ch), *1 cluster into next 2-ch sp, ch 2, rep from * ending, 1 cluster into last sp, 1 dc in 3rd of 5 ch, turn.

Row 9 Ch 5, * 1 cluster into next 2-ch sp, ch 2, rep from * ending 1 cluster into last sp, 1 dc into top of 3 ch, turn.

Row 10 Ch 3, 1 dc into top of first cluster, * 2 dc into 2-ch sp, 1 dc into top of next cluster, rep from * ending, 2 dc into last sp, 1 dc into 3rd of 5 ch, turn.

Rows 2–10 form patt.
Patt 18 more rows.

Shape side

Keeping patt correct, dc3tog at beg of next row, foll 8th row, 2 foll 6th rows, then 3 foll 4th rows. 45 (51:57) sts.

Shape front

Keeping side edge straight, work dc3tog at beg of next and foll 4 alt rows. 35 (41:47) sts.

Shape armhole

Row 71 Ss across and into 10th (11th:12th) st, patt to end, turn. 26 (31:36) sts.

Rows 72 and 74 Dc3tog, patt to last 2 sts, dc2tog, turn.

Rows 73 and 75 Dc2tog, patt to end, turn. 18 (23:28) sts.

Patt 2 rows.

Row 78 Dc3tog, patt to end, turn.

Patt 3 rows.

Row 82 Dc3tog, patt to end, turn. 14 (19:24) sts.

Patt 5 (7:9) rows. Fasten off.

SLEEVES

Ch 53 (59:65).

Row 1 (RS) 1 dc into 4th ch from hook, 1 dc into each ch to end, turn.

51 (57:63) sts.

Row 2 Ch 4 (counts as 1 dc and 1 ch), skip first 2 dc, *1 dc into next dc, ch 1, skip next dc, rep from * to end, 1 dc in top of 3 ch, turn. 25 (28:31) squares.

Cont in patt as given for Back. Patt another 11 (10:9) rows. Inc 1 st at each end of the next and 3 (5:2) foll 4th (4th:3rd) rows, then on the 2 (1:5) foll 6th (5th:4th) rows. 63 (71:79) sts.

Patt another 5 rows, ending with a 7th patt row.

Shape top

Next row Ss across and into the 10th (11th:12th) st, patt to last 9 (10:11) sts, turn. 45 (51:57) sts.

Patt 1 row.

Next row Dc3tog, patt to the last 3 sts, dc3tog, turn.

Rep last 2 rows once more, then patt 1 row. 37 (43:49) sts.

Next row Dc2tog, patt to the last 2 sts, dc2tog, turn.

Rep the last row 5 (7:9) more times. 25 (27:29) sts. Fasten off.

FINISHING

Join shoulders.

Set in sleeves.

Join side and sleeve seams. Weave in all yarn ends.

Lower border

With RS facing, join yarn at lower corner of Left Front.

Row 1 Ch 1 (counts as 1 sc), work a row of sc evenly along lower edge, so that there are a multiple of 6 sts plus 1, turn.

Row 2 Ch 8 (count as 1 dc, 5 ch), skip first 6 sc, 1 dc into next sc, * ch 5, skip 5 sc, 1 dc into next sc; rep from * to end, turn.

Row 3 Ch 6 (count as 1 tr, 2 ch), work 1 bobble into first dc, * into next dc work [1 bobble, ch 5, 1 bobble]; rep from * ending [1 bobble, ch 2, 1 tr], into 6th of 8 ch, turn.

Row 4 Ch 1, 1 sc into first tr, * ch 7, 1 sc into next 5-ch arch; rep from * ending ch 7, 1 sc into 3rd of 6 ch, turn.

Row 5 Ch 1, 1 sc into first sc, *9 sc into next 7-ch arch, 1 sc into next sc; rep from * to end. Fasten off. Weave in yarn ends.

Cuffs (both alike)

With RS facing, join yarn at sleeve seam.

Round 1 Ch 1 (counts as 1 sc), work in sc evenly along cuff edge so that there are a multiple of 6 sts, ss to first ch, turn.

Round 2 Ch 8 (count as 1 dc, 5 ch), skip first 6 sc, * 1 dc into next sc, ch 5, skip 5 sc, rep from * ending ss to 3rd of 8 ch, turn.

Round 3 Ch 6 (count as 1 tr, 2 ch), work as given for Row 3 on lower border ending ss to 4th of 6 ch, turn.

Round 4 Ch 1, 1 sc into first tr, work as given for 4th row on lower border, ending ss to 1 ch, turn.

Round 5 Ch 1, 1 sc into first sc, work as given for 5th row on lower border, ending ss to 1 ch. Fasten off. Weave in yarn ends.

Front edge

With RS facing, join yarn to lower right border.

Row 1 Ch 1 (counts as 1 sc), work in sc evenly around front edges, turn.

Row 2 Ch 1 (counts as 1 sc), 1 sc in each sc, ending 1 sc in 1 ch, Fasten off. Weave in yarn ends.

Cords (make 2)

Ch 100. Fasten off. Weave in yarn ends.

Attach a cord to each front edge at beg of front shaping.

Chevron Classic

This eye-catching halter top is worked in a soft cotton yarn. The diagonal stripes on the front section are formed by increasing at the center and decreasing at the sides. The back is worked in horizontal stripes using simple double crochet stitches.

Skill level: ADVANCED

MEASUREMENTS

To fit bust

32	34	36	38	in.
81	86	91	97	cm

Actual width

31	33	35	37	in.
78	84	89	94	cm

Length of side seam

10¼	10¾	11	11½	in.
26	27	28	29	cm

MATERIALS

- 1 (1:1:2) × 100 g (3½ oz.) balls of Sirdar Breeze DK in Sage 047 (A)

- 1 × 100 g (3½ oz.) ball of Sirdar Breeze DK in Khaki 048 (B)

- 1 × 100 g (3½ oz.) ball of Sirdar Breeze DK in Corn 046 (C)

- G/6 (4.25 mm) crochet hook

GAUGE

16 dc and 10 rows to 4 in. (10 cm) measured over double crochet pattern using G/6 (4.25 mm) crochet hook. Change hook size, if necessary, to obtain this gauge.

ABBREVIATIONS

sc2tog—[insert hook into next st, yoh and pull through a loop] twice, yoh and pull through all 3 loops on hook, To dec 1 st.
See also page 11.

NOTE

Figures in parentheses refer to the larger sizes; where only one set of figures is given, this refers to all sizes.

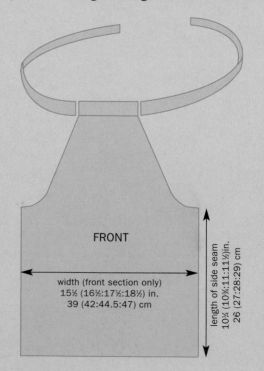

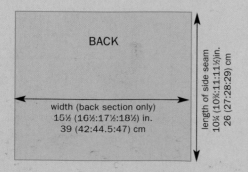

BACK

width (back section only)
15½ (16½:17½:18½) in.
39 (42:44.5:47) cm

length of side seam
10¼ (10¾:11:11½)in.
26 (27:28:29) cm

FRONT

width (front section only)
15½ (16½:17½:18½) in.
39 (42:44.5:47) cm

length of side seam
10¼ (10¾:11:11½)in.
26 (27:28:29) cm

HALTER TOP

FRONT

Using A, ch 7.

Foundation row With A, work 1 dc into 4th ch from hook, 2 dc in each of rem 3 ch, turn. 8 sts.

Row 1 With B, ch 3 (counts as 1 dc), 1 dc into base of 3 ch just worked, 1 dc into each of next 2 dc, (3 dc into next dc) twice, 1 dc into each of next 2 dc, 2 dc into top of tch, turn. 14 sts.

Row 2 With C, ch 3 (counts as 1 dc), 1 dc into base of 3 ch just worked, 1 dc into each of next 5 dc, (3 dc into next dc) twice, 1 dc into each of next 5 dc, 2 dc into tch, turn. 20 sts.

Row 3 With A, ch 3 (counts as 1 dc), 1 dc into base of 3 ch just worked, 1 dc into each of next 8 dc, (3 dc into next dc) twice, 1 dc into each of next 8 dc, 2 dc into top of tch, turn. 26 sts.

Row 4 With B, ch 3 (counts as 1 dc), 1 dc into base of 3 ch just worked, 1 dc into each of next 11 dc, (3 dc into next dc) twice, 1 dc into each of next 11 dc, 2 dc into top of tch, turn. 32 sts.

Row 5 With C, ch 3 (counts as 1 dc), 1 dc into base of 3 ch just worked, 1 dc into each of next 14 dc, (3 dc into next dc) twice, 1 dc into each of next 14 dc, 2 dc into top of tch, turn. 38 sts.

Row 6 With A, ch 3 (counts as 1 dc), 1 dc into base of 3 ch just worked, 1 dc into each of next 17 dc, (3 dc into next dc) twice, 1 dc into each of next 17 dc, 2 dc into top of tch, turn. 44 sts.

Cont in patt and stripe sequence as now set, working incs in same position on every row, adding 3 extra double crochet on each side, until the following row has been worked:

Next row Ch 3 (counts as 1 dc), 1 dc into base of 3 ch just worked, 1 dc into each of next 44 (47:50:53) dc, (3 dc into next dc) twice, 1 dc into each of next 44 (47:50:53) dc, 2 dc into top of tch, turn. 98 (104:110:116) sts.

The top is fastened with a simple tie at the neck.

Work sides

Next row Ss across 2 dc, 1 sc into each of next 2 dc, 1 hdc into each of next 2 dc, 1 dc into each of next 42 (45:48:51) dc, (3 dc into next dc) twice, 1 dc into each of next 42 (45:48:51) dc, 1 hdc into each of next 2 dc, 1 sc into each of next 2 dc, ss to next dc, turn. 98 (104:110:116) sts.

Next row Ss across 2 sc, 1 sc into each of 2 hdc, 1 hdc into each of next 2 dc, 1 dc into each of next 42 (45:48:51) dc, (3 dc into next dc) twice, 1 dc into each of next 42 (45:48:51) dc, 1 hdc into each of next 2 dc, 1 sc into each of next 2 hdc, ss to next sc, turn. 98 (104:110:116) sts.

Rep this last row 10 (11,12:13) more times.

Next row Ss in next sc, 1 sc in next sc, 1 dc into each of next 2 hdc, 1 tr into each of the next 2 dc, (place a marker on last tr for side seam), 1 dc into each of the next 41 (44:47:50) dc, 1 hdc in next dc, 1 sc in each of next 6 dc, 1 hdc in next dc, 1 dc into each of the next 41 (44:47:50) dc, 1 tr into each of the next 2 dc (place a marker in first tr for side seam), 1 dc into each of the next 2 hdc, 1 sc in next sc, ss to next sc. Fasten off. Mark center 4 sc at top. 100 (103:106:109) sts.

Side seam measures approximately 8¾ (9:9½:10) in. (22 [23:24:25] cm) from beg.

BACK

Using C, ch 64 (69:73:77).

Foundation row 1 dc into 4th ch from hook, 1 dc in each ch to end. 62 (67:71:75) sts.

Row 1 With A, ch 3 (counts as 1 dc), 1 dc into each st ending 1 dc in top of tch, turn.

Row 2 With B, work as given for first row.

Row 3 With C, work as given for first row.

These 3 rows form the pattern. Cont in patt until work measures same as Front to marker for side seam. Fasten off.

LOWER EDGE

Join side seams.

With RS facing, join A at one side seam.

Foundation round Ch 1 (counts as 1 sc), work sc evenly around lower edge, ss to 1ch, turn.

Next round Ch 1 (counts as 1 sc), 1 sc in each sc, ss to 1 ch, turn.

Work 3 more rounds in sc. Fasten off.

FRONT AND BACK EDGE

With RS facing, join A to next sc after marker at right front neck, ch 1 (counts as 1 sc), work sc evenly down right front, across back, and up left front, ending 1 sc in sc before marker, turn.

Next row Ch 1 (counts as 1 sc), sc2tog, 1 sc in each sc to last 3 sts, sc2tog, 1 sc in tch, turn.

Rep this row 3 more times.

TOP NECKBAND

With RS facing and using A, ch 1 (counts as 1 sc), work in sc along top edge, turn.

Next row Ch 1 (counts as 1 sc), 1 sc in each sc, 1 sc in tch, turn.

Rep this last row 11 more times. Fasten off.

Fold top edge over to WS and ss down to first row.

NECK TIE

Using C, ch 138.

Next row 1 sc into 2nd ch from hook, 1 sc in each ch to end. 137 sts.

Next row Ch 1 (counts as 1 sc), 1 sc in each sc, 1 sc in tch, turn.

Rep the last row 2 more times. Fasten off.

FINISHING

Thread neck tie through top neckband. Weave in all yarn ends.

Casual Comfort Jacket

The simple design of this jacket, in a soft brushed chunky yarn, makes this a quick and easy garment to crochet. On cool days it is just the right choice for staying both comfortable and warm.

Skill level: INTERMEDIATE

MEASUREMENTS

To fit bust

32–34	36–38	40–42	in.
81–86	91–97	102–107	cm

Actual width

41½	45½	50	in.
105	115	127	cm

Length from shoulder

23	23¼	23½	in.
58	59	60	cm

Sleeve seam

18	18	18½	in.
46	46	47	cm

MATERIALS

- 7 (8:9) × 85 g (3 oz.) balls of Lion Jiffy in Violet 191

- K/10½ (6.50 mm) and J/10 (6.00 mm) crochet hooks

- 5 buttons, ⅞ in. (2 cm) in diameter

GAUGE

9 sts and 7½ rows to 4 in. (10 cm) measured over half double crochet pattern using K/10½ (6.50 mm) crochet hook. Change hook size, if necessary, to obtain this gauge.

ABBREVIATIONS

hdc2(3)tog—leaving last loop of each st on hook, work 1 hdc into each of the next 2 (3) sts, yoh and draw through rem 3 (4) loops to dec 1 (2) sts.
See also page 11.

NOTE
Figures in parentheses refer to the larger sizes; where only one set of figures is given, this refers to all sizes.

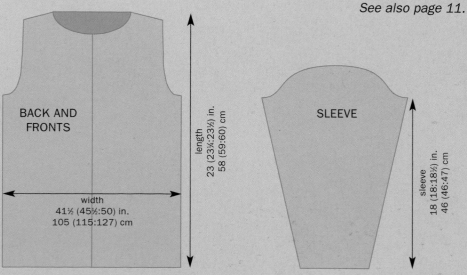

BACK AND FRONTS

width
41½ (45½:50) in.
105 (115:127) cm

length
23 (23¼:23½) in.
58 (59:60) cm

SLEEVE

sleeve
18 (18:18½) in.
46 (46:47) cm

JACKET

BACK

Using larger hook, ch 48 (53:58).

Foundation row (RS) 1 hdc into 3rd ch from hook,
1 hdc in each ch to end, turn. 47 (52:57) sts.

Row 1 Ch (counts as 1 hdc), 1 hdc into each st ending
1 hdc in tch, turn.

Rep this row until work measures 15 in. (38 cm)
from beg.

This simple jacket is perfect for cooler days.

Shape armholes

Row 1 Ss across and into 3rd (4th:5th) st, ch 2 (counts
as 1 hdc), 1 hdc in each st to last 2 (3:4) sts, turn.
43 (46:49) sts.

Row 2 Ch 2 (counts as 1 hdc), hdc2tog, 1hdc in each st
to last 3 sts, hdc2tog, 1 hdc in tch, turn.

Rep last row 3 more times. 35 (38:41) sts.

Cont straight until armholes measure 8 (8¼:8¾) in.
(20 [21:22] cm) from beg.

Shape shoulders

Next row Ss across and into 6th (7th:7th) st, ch 2

(counts as 1 hdc), 1 hdc in each st to last 5 (6:6) sts, turn. Fasten off.

Mark the center 15 (16:17) sts for back neck.

LEFT FRONT

Using larger hook, ch 27 (29:32).

Foundation row (RS) 1 hdc into 3rd ch from hook, 1 hdc in each ch to end, turn. 26 (28:31) sts.

Cont as Back until work measures 15 in. (38 cm) from beg.

Shape armhole

Row 1 Ss across and into 3rd (4th:5th) st, ch 2 (counts as 1 hdc), 1 hdc in each st ending 1 hdc in tch, turn. 24 (25:27) sts.

Rows 2 and 4 Ch 2 (counts as 1 hdc), 1 hdc into each st to last 3 sts, hdc2tog, 1 hdc in tch, turn.

Rows 3 and 5 Ch 2 (counts as 1 hdc), hdc2tog, 1 hdc in each st ending 1 hdc in tch, turn. 20 (21:23) sts.

Cont straight until front measures 5 rows fewer than back to shoulder shaping, ending at front edge.

Shape neck

Row 1 Ss across and into 7th (7th:8th) st, ch 2 (counts as 1 hdc), 1 hdc in each st ending 1 hdc in tch, turn. 14 (15:16) sts.

Rows 2 and 4 Ch 2 (counts as 1 hdc), 1 hdc in each st to last 3 sts, hdc2tog, 1 hdc in tch, turn.

Rows 3 and 5 Ch 2 (counts as 1 hdc), hdc2tog, 1 hdc in each st ending 1 hdc in tch, turn. 10 (11:12) sts.

Shape shoulder

Next row Ss across and into 6th (7th:7th) st, ch 2 (counts as 1 hdc), 1 hdc in each st ending 1 hdc in tch. 5 (5:6) sts. Fasten off.

Mark positions of 5 buttons, the first 4 in. (10 cm) up from lower edge of front, the last ¾ in. (2 cm) down from neck edge, the rem 3 spaced evenly between.

RIGHT FRONT

Work as given for Left Front, making buttonholes to correspond with markers by substituting 3rd hdc from front edge with ch 1, skip 3rd hdc on each appropriate row. Complete to match Left Front, reversing shapings.

SLEEVES

Using larger hook, ch 25 (27:28).

Foundation row (RS) 1 hdc into 3rd ch from hook, 1 hdc in each ch to end. 24 (26:27) sts.

Cont as Back, inc 1 st at each end of 3rd (2nd:2nd) row and 5 (1:9) foll 4th (3rd:3rd) rows. 36 (30:47) sts. Inc 1 st at each end of 1 (6:0) foll 6th (4th:0) rows. 38 (42:47) sts. Cont straight until Sleeve measures 17¾ (17¾:18) in. (45 [45:46] cm) from beg.

Shape top

Row 1 Ss across and into 3rd (4th:5th) st, ch 2 (counts as 1 hdc), 1 hdc in each st to last 2 (3:4) sts, turn. 34 (36:39) sts.

Row 2 Ch 2 (counts as 1 hdc), hdc2tog, 1 hdc in each st to the last 3 sts, hdc2tog, 1 hdc in tch, turn.

Rep last row 5 (6:7) more times. 22 (22:23) sts.

Next row Ch 2 (counts as 1 hdc), hdc3tog, 1 hdc in each st to last 4 sts, hdc3tog, 1 hdc in tch, turn.

Rep last row 2 more times. 10 (10:11) sts. Fasten off.

FINISHING

Join shoulders. Set in sleeves.

Join side and sleeve seams. Weave in all yarn ends.

Edging

Using smaller hook, join yarn at right side seam.

Round 1 Ch 1, work in sc evenly around entire outer edge, working 2 sc into each corner on lower fronts and neck edge, ss to 1 ch at beg.

Round 2 Ch 1, work 1 sc in each sc, with 2 sc into each corner, ss to 1 ch at beg. Fasten off. Weave in yarn ends.

Cuffs

Using smaller hook, join yarn at sleeve seam.

Round 1 Ch 1, work in sc evenly around cuff edge, ss to 1 ch at beg.

Round 2 Ch 1, work 1 sc in each sc, ss to 1 ch at beg. Fasten off. Weave in yarn ends.

Buttons

Sew 5 buttons to Left Front.

Lacy Openwork Tunic

This tunic is worked in a lightweight cotton yarn. The allover pattern is a bit challenging, but the end result is worth the effort. Pair it with a camisole for a springtime fashion favorite.

★★★

Skill level: ADVANCED

MEASUREMENTS

To fit bust

34	36	38	40	in.
86	91	97	102	cm

Actual width

36	39½	42½	45½	in.
92	100	108	116	cm

Length from shoulder

29½	30½	31	31	in.
75	77	79	79	cm

Sleeve seam

8½ in. (21 cm)

MATERIALS

- 3 (4:4:5) × 100 g (3½ oz.) balls of Sirdar Cotton 4-ply in White 029

- C/2 (2.50 mm) crochet hook

GAUGE

3 flower-and-cross patt repeats measure 4¾ in. (12 cm) in width, and the 8-row patt repeat measures 3 in. (8 cm) in depth, using C/2 (2.50 mm) crochet hook. Change hook size, if necessary, to obtain this gauge.

ABBREVIATIONS

tr2tog—leaving last loop of each tr on hook, work 2 tr in next st, yoh and draw through all 3 loops.
See also page 11.

NOTE

Figures in parentheses refer to the larger sizes; where only one set of figures is given, this refers to all sizes.

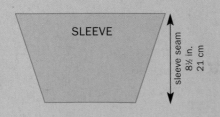

SLEEVE

sleeve seam
8½ in.
21 cm

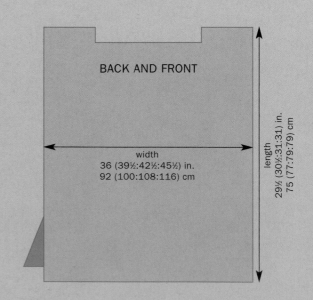

BACK AND FRONT

width
36 (39½:42½:45½) in.
92 (100:108:116) cm

length
29½ (30½:31:31) in.
75 (77:79:79) cm

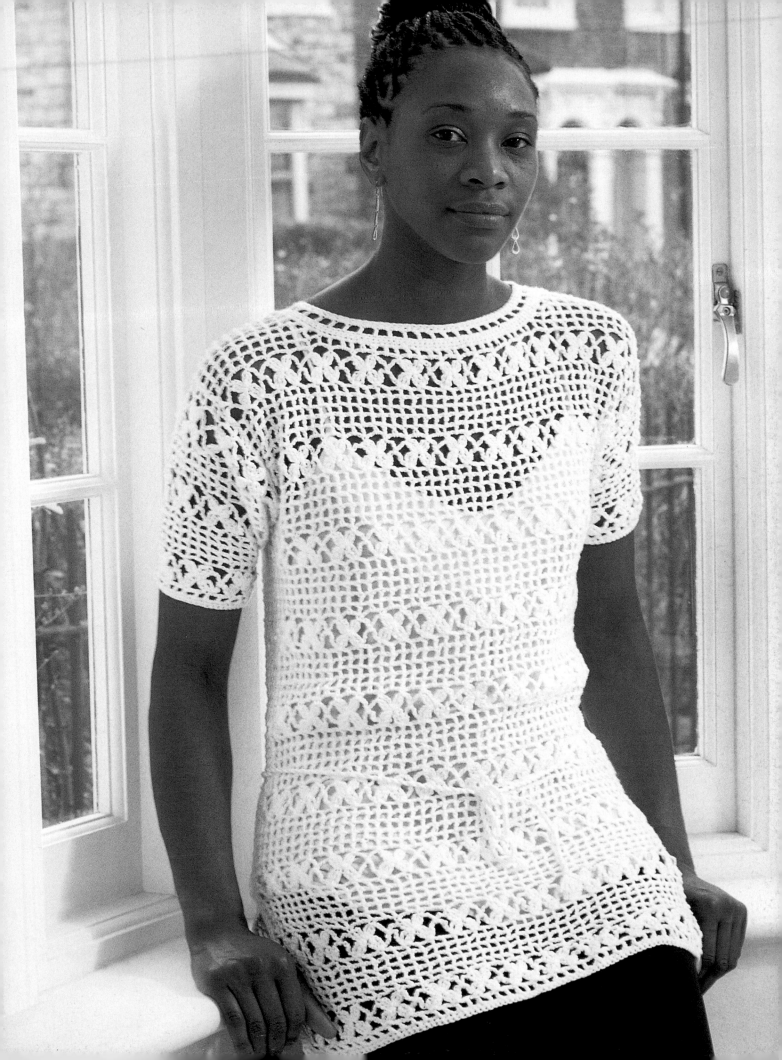

TUNIC

BACK AND FRONT (make 2 alike)

Ch 143 (155:167:179).

Foundation row (RS) Work 1 dc into 8th ch from hook, *ch 2, skip 2 ch, 1dc into next ch; rep from * to end, turn. 46 (50:54:58) squares.

Row 1 Ch 1, 1 sc into first dc, *ch 9, skip 1 dc, into next dc work [1 sc, ch 4, tr2tog], skip 1 dc, into next dc work [tr2tog, ch 4, 1 sc]; rep from * to last 2 squares, ch 9, skip 1 dc, 1 sc into 3rd of 8 ch, turn.

Row 2 Ch 10 (count as 1 trtr, 4 ch), 1 sc into first 9-ch arch, *ch 4, into top of next tr2tog work [tr2tog, ch 4, 1 ss, ch 4, tr2tog], ch 4, 1 sc into next 9-ch arch; rep from * ending ch 4, 1 trtr into last sc, turn. 11 (12:13:14) cross-and-flower patts plus 1 cross.

Row 3 Ch 1, 1 sc into first trtr, *ch 5, 1 sc into top of next tr2tog; rep from * to end, placing last sc into 5th of 10 ch, turn.

Row 4 Ch 5 (count as 1 dc, 2 ch), 1 dc into center ch of next 5-ch arch, ch 2, 1 dc into next sc, *ch 2, 1 dc into center ch of next 5-ch arch, ch 2, 1 dc into next sc; rep from * to end, turn. 46 (50:54:58) squares.

Rows 5–8 Ch 5 (count as 1 dc, 2 ch), skip first dc, *1 dc into next dc, ch 2, rep from * ending 1 dc in 3rd of 5 ch, turn.

Rep Rows 1–8 seven times, then work Rows 1–4 again.

Work 0 (2:4:4) more rows in filet as Rows 5–8.

Shape neck

Next row Patt 11 (12:13:14) squares, turn, and work on these sts for first side.

Dec row 1 Ch 3, skip first dc and 2 ch, 1 dc in next dc; *ch 2, 1 dc in next dc; rep from * ending ch 2, 1 dc in 3rd of 5 ch, turn.

Dec row 2 Ch 5 (count as 1 dc, 2 ch), 1 dc into next dc, *ch 2, 1 dc into next dc, rep from * to last full square, skip 2 ch, 1 dc in next dc, turn. 9 (10:11:12) squares.

Next row Ch 5 (count as 1 dc, 2 ch) skip first 2 dc, *1 dc into next dc, ch 2, rep from * ending 1 dc in 3rd of 5 ch. 9 (10:11:12) squares.

Next row As Row 5. Fasten off.

Return to rem sts. Leave the center 24 (26:28:30) squares, rejoining yarn to last dc on last square, work ch 5 (count as 1 dc, 2 ch), *1 dc into next dc, ch 2, rep from * ending 1 dc in 3rd of 5 ch. 11 (12:13:14) squares. Complete as given for first side, reversing shapings.

SLEEVES (make 2)

Ch 83 (95:107:119).

Foundation row (RS) 1 dc into 8th ch from hook, *ch 2, skip 2 ch, 1 dc into next ch; rep from * to end, turn. 26 (30:34:38) squares.

Rows 1–4 Work as given for Back. 6 (7:8:9) cross-and-flower patts plus 1 cross.

Row 5 (inc row) Ch 5 (counts as 1 dc and 2 ch), 1 dc into first dc, *ch 2, 1 dc in next dc; rep from * ending (ch 2, 1 dc) twice into 3rd of 5 ch, turn. 28 (32:36:40) squares.

Row 6 Ch 5 (counts as 1 dc and 2 ch), skip first dc, *1 dc into next dc, ch 2, rep from * ending 1 dc in 3rd of 5 ch, turn.

Rep last 2 rows once more. 30 (34:38:42) squares.

Row 9 (inc row) Ch 1, into first dc work [1 sc, ch 4, 1 tr, ch 4, 1 sc], *ch 9, skip 1 dc, into next dc work [1 sc, ch 4, tr2tog], skip 1 dc, into next dc work [tr2tog, ch 4, 1sc] rep from * to last 2 squares, ch 9, skip 1 dc, into 3rd of 5 ch work [1 sc, ch 4, tr2tog], turn.

Row 10 (inc row) Into first tr2tog work [ch 4, 1 tr, ch 4, 1 ss, ch 4, tr2tog,] *ch 4, 1 sc into 9-ch arch, ch 4, into top of next tr2tog work [tr2tog, ch 4, 1 ss, ch 4, tr2tog]; rep from * to end. 8 (9:10:11) flower patts.

Row 11 Ch 1, 1 sc in top of first tr2tog, *ch 5, 1 sc in top of next tr2tog; rep from * to end, turn.

Rows 12–16 Rep Rows 4–8.

Rows 17–20 As Rows 1–4. Fasten off.

NECKBAND

Join shoulders. Join yarn to 2-ch sp at shoulder seam.

Round 1 (RS) Ch 1 (counts as 1 sc), 1 sc in same ch sp, work 2 sc into each ch sp all round neck edge plus 1 extra sc in center of front and back (back:0:front and back). 116 (124:132:140) sts. Ss to 1 ch, turn.

Rounds 2 and 3 Ch 1 (counts as 1 sc), 1 sc in each st to end, ss to 1 ch, turn.

Round 4 Ch 5 (counts as 1 dc and 2 ch), skip 2 sts, *1 dc in next st, ch 2, skip 2 sts; rep from * ending ss to 3rd of 5 ch, turn.

Round 5 Ch 1 (counts as 1 sc), 1 sc in same ch sp, then work 2 sc in each 2-ch sp to end, ss to 1 ch, turn.

Round 6 Ch 1 (counts as 1 sc), 1 sc in each sc to end, ss to 1 ch. Fasten off.

FINISHING

Mark side edges 7½ (8¼:9:9¾) in. (19 [21:23:25] cm) down from each shoulder. Fold sleeve in half lengthwise to find midpoint. Place the midpoint of the sleeve at shoulder seam; sew sleeves between markers.

Join sleeve seams, then sides, leaving last 6½ in. (16 cm) for side slits at bottom of garment. Weave in yarn ends.

Lower border

With RS facing, join yarn to top of one side slit.

Round 1 Ch 1, then work in sc evenly along side slits and lower edges, ss to 1 ch, turn.

Round 2 Ch 1, work 1 sc into each sc to end, working 3 sc into sc at each corner and skipping top sc at each side of both slits, ss to first ch. Fasten off. Weave in yarn ends.

Cuffs

With RS facing, join yarn to sleeve seam.

Round 1 Ch 1, work sc evenly along cuff edge, ss to 1 ch, turn.

Round 2 Ch 1, work 1 sc in each sc to end, ss to 1 ch. Fasten off. Weave in yarn ends.

BELT (optional)

Make a twisted cord by cutting two or three strands of yarn to double the desired length of the finished cord. Knot together at each end and attach one end to a hook. Insert a knitting needle through the other end and turn clockwise until the strands are tightly twisted. Holding the cord in the center, bring the two ends together so that the two halves twist together. Trim the ends and tie around waist.

This openwork tunic looks great over a simple camisole.

Tunic with Lace Borders

The main body and sleeves of this lightweight cotton tunic are worked in simple double crochet stitches with an attractive lacy border on the front, back, and sleeves. Wear this sweater with a belt over jeans or a skirt or as a casual beach cover-up.

Skill level: ADVANCED

MEASUREMENTS

To fit bust

32–34	36	38	40–42	in.
81–86	91	97	102–107	cm

Actual width

38	40	43½	46	in.
95	102	110	117	cm

Length from shoulder

27	27½	28½	28½	in.
68	70	72	72	cm

Sleeve seam

18 in. (46 cm)

MATERIALS

• 12 (13:14:15) × 50 g (1¾ oz.) balls of Rowan 4-ply Cotton in Bluebell 136

• C/2 (2.75 mm) and D/3 (3.25 mm) crochet hooks

GAUGE

22 sts and 13 rows to 4 in. (10 cm) measured over double crochet pattern, using C/2 (2.75 mm) crochet hook. Change hook size, if necessary, to obtain this gauge.

ABBREVIATIONS

inc—increase at beg of row by working ch 3, 1 dc into same st; inc at end of row by working 2 dc into the same st.

bobble—leaving last loop of each st on hook, work 4 dc into next st, yoh and draw through all 5 loops.

dc3tog—leaving last loop of each st on hook, work 1 dc into each of next 3 dc, yoh and draw through all 4 loops to dec 2 sts.

sc2tog—[insert hook in next st, yoh and draw loop through] twice, yoh and draw through all 3 loops to dec 1 st.

See also page 11.

NOTES

Figures in parentheses refer to the larger sizes; where only one set of figures is given, this refers to all sizes.

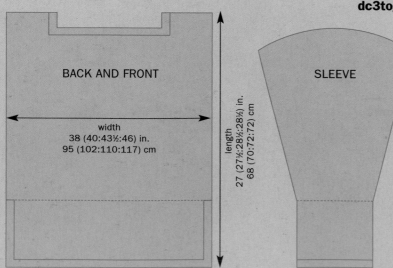

BACK AND FRONT

width
38 (40:43½:46) in.
95 (102:110:117) cm

length
27 (27½:28½:28½) in.
68 (70:72:72) cm

SLEEVE

sleeve
18 in.
46 cm

SWEATER

BACK AND FRONT (both alike)

Using smaller hook, ch 106 (114:122:130).

Hem edge

Foundation row (WS) 1 sc into 2nd ch from hook, 1 sc into each ch to end, turn. 105 (113:121:129) sts.

Next row Ch 1 (counts as 1 sc), 1 sc in each sc, 1 sc in tch, turn.

Rep last row 2 more times.

Border pattern

Change to larger hook. Cont in border patt as follows:

Row 1 (WS) Ch 4 (counts as 1 dc, 1 ch), skip the next st, 1 bobble into next st, ch 1, skip 1 st, 1 dc into next st, *ch 1, skip 1 st, 1 bobble into next st, ch 1, skip

1 st, 1 dc into next st; rep from * to end, turn.

Row 2 Ch 2 (counts as first hdc), work 1 hdc into each dc, ch sp, and bobble to end, ending 1 hdc into last ch sp, 1 hdc into 3rd of 4 ch, turn.

Row 3 Ch 1, 1 sc into each of first 3 sc, *ch 5, skip 3 sc, 1 sc into each of next 5 sc; rep from * to end omitting 2 sc at end of last rep, turn.

Row 4 Ch 1, 1 sc into each of first 2 sc, *ch 3, 1 sc into 5-ch arch, ch 3, skip 1 sc, 1 sc into each of next 3 sc; rep from * to end, omitting 1 sc at end of last rep, turn.

Row 5 Ch 1, 1 sc into first sc, *ch 3, 1 sc into next 3-ch arch, 1 sc into next sc, 1 sc into next 3-ch arch, ch 3, skip 1 sc, 1 sc into next sc; rep from * to end, turn.

Row 6 Ch 5 (count as 1 dc, 2 ch), 1 sc into next 3-ch arch, 1 sc into each of next 3 sc, 1 sc into next 3-ch arch, *ch 5, 1 sc into next 3-ch arch, 1 sc into each of next 3 sc, 1 sc into next 3-ch arch; rep from * to last sc, ch 2, 1 dc into last sc, turn.

Row 7 Ch 1, 1 sc into first dc, *ch 3, skip 1 sc, 1 sc into each of next 3 sc, ch 3, 1 sc into next 5-ch arch; rep from * to end placing last sc into 3rd of 5 ch at beg of previous row, turn.

Row 8 Ch 1, 1 sc into first sc, *1 sc into next 3-ch arch, ch 3, skip 1 sc, 1 sc into next sc, ch 3, 1 sc into next 3-ch arch, 1 sc into next sc; rep from * to end, turn.

Row 9 Ch 1, 1 sc into each of first 2 sc, *1 sc into next 3-ch arch, ch 3, 1 sc into next 3-ch arch, 1 sc into each of next 3 sc; rep from * to end omitting 1 sc at end of last rep, turn.

Row 10 Ch 2 (count as first hdc), 1 hdc into each of next 2 sc, *3 hdc into next 3-ch arch, 1 hdc into each of next 5 sc; rep from * to end omitting 2 sc at end of last rep, turn.

Row 11 Ch 4 (count as 1 dc, ch 1), skip next hdc, 1 bobble into next hdc, ch 1, skip 1 hdc, 1 dc into next hdc, *ch 1, skip 1 hdc, 1 bobble into next hdc, ch 1, skip 1 hdc, 1 dc into next hdc; rep from * to end, turn.

Row 12 As Row 2. 105 (113:121:129) sts.

Rep Rows 1–12 twice more.

These 36 rows complete border.

Change to smaller hook. Cont in main patt as follows:

The attractive lacy border adds a special touch.

Next row Ch 3 (counts as 1 dc), 1 dc in each st ending 1 dc in tch, turn.

Rep this row throughout until work measures 25 (26:27:27) in. (64 [66:68:68] cm) from beg.

Shape neck

Row 1 Ch 3 (counts as 1 dc), 1 dc in each of next 39 (41:43:45) dc, turn and work on these 40 (42:44:46) sts for the first side.

Row 2 Ch 3 (counts as 1 dc), dc3tog, 1 dc in each dc ending 1 dc in tch, turn.

Row 3 Ch 3 (counts as 1 dc), 1 dc in each dc to last 4 sts, dc3tog, 1 dc in tch, turn.

Rep the last 2 rows once more, then Row 2 again. 30 (32:34:36) sts.

Leave the center 25 (29:33:37) sts, rejoin yarn to next st, ch 3 (counts as 1 dc), 1 dc in each dc ending 1 dc in tch, turn.

Complete to match first side, reversing shapings.

SLEEVES

Using smaller hook, ch 58 (66:66:74).

Hem edge

Foundation row 1 sc into 2nd ch from hook, 1 sc in each ch to end. 57 (65:65:73) sts.

Next row Ch 1 (counts as 1 sc), 1 sc in each sc, ending 1 sc in tch, turn.

Rep the last row 2 more times.

Border pattern

Change to larger hook. Work 36 rows in border patt as given for Back.

Change to smaller hook. Cont in main patt as follows:

Next row Ch 3 (counts as 1 dc), 1 dc in each st ending 1 dc in tch, turn.

Rep this row throughout, inc 1 st at each end of the next 8 rows. 73 (81:81:89) sts.

[Work 1 row, then inc 1 st at each end of next 2 rows] 5 times. 93 (101:101:109) sts.

Cont straight until Sleeve measures 18 in. (46 cm) from beg.

Shape top

Next row Ss across and into the 11th (12th:12th:13th) st, ch 3 (counts as 1 dc), 1 dc in each st to the last 10 (11:11:12) sts, turn.

Rep last row 3 more times. 13 sts. Fasten off.

NECKBAND

Join shoulders.

With RS facing and using smaller hook, rejoin yarn to one shoulder. Ch 1 (counts as 1 sc), work in sc evenly around neck edge so that there is a multiple of 4 sts, ss to 1 ch at beg of round, turn.

Next round Ch 4 (counts as 1 dc and 1 ch), skip next sc, *1 bobble into next sc, ch 1, skip next sc, 1 dc in next sc, ch 1, skip next sc; rep from * omitting 1 dc and ch on the last rep, ss to 3rd of 4 ch, turn.

Next round Ch 1 (counts as 1 sc), 1 sc in each dc, ch sp, and bobble, ss to 1 ch. Fasten off.

FINISHING

Mark positions 8½ (9½:9½:10¼) in. (22 [24:24:26] cm) down from each side of shoulder seam. Fold sleeves in half lengthwise, and placing center point at shoulder seams, sew between markers on back and front.

Join sleeve seams. Starting at Row 34 of border, join side seams to underarms. Weave in yarn ends.

Side slits

With RS facing and using smaller hook, rejoin yarn at lower corner of Right Front.

Row 1 Ch 1 (counts as 1 sc), work in sc along one side of the slit, 1 sc into seam, and mark this st, work same number of sc along other side slit, turn.

Row 2 Ch 1 (counts as 1 sc), work 1 sc in each sc to within 2 sts of marked st, sc2tog, 1 sc in marked st, sc2tog, 1 sc in each st to end, turn.

Rows 3 and 4 As Row 2. Fasten off. Repeat for second slit. Weave in yarn ends.

Bolero Sizzle

You'll get noticed in this fashionable bolero, which is worked in a bright cotton yarn. The back, fronts, and sleeves are worked up to the armhole; then, working in rows across all the pieces allows you to form a yoke and shape the neck easily.

Skill level: INTERMEDIATE

MEASUREMENTS

To fit bust

32	34	36	38	in.
81	86	91	97	cm

Actual width

33½	36	38	40½	in.
85	91	97	103	cm

Length from back neck

15	15½	16	17	in.
38	39	41	43	cm

Sleeve seam

6¼ in. (16 cm)

MATERIALS

- 3 (3:4:5) × 140 g (5 oz.) balls of Lion Cotton in Turquoise 148
- G/6 (4.25 mm) and 7 (4.50 mm) crochet hooks

GAUGE

13 sts and 13½ rows to 4 in. (10 cm) measured over pattern, using 7 (4.50 mm) crochet hook. Change hook size, if necessary, to obtain this gauge.

ABBREVIATIONS

inc—increase by working 2 sc or 2 hdc into next st (work ch 1 for 1 sc; ch 2 for 1hdc, for first sc or hdc at beg of row).

sc2tog—[insert hook in next sc, yoh and draw loop through] twice, yoh and draw through all 3 loops, to dec 1 st.
See also page 11.

NOTE

Figures in parentheses refer to the larger sizes; where only one set of figures is given, this refers to all sizes.

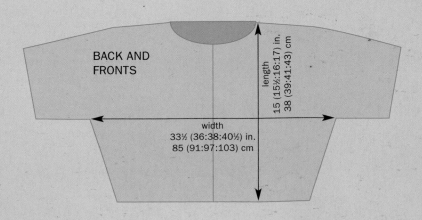

BACK AND FRONTS

length
15 (15½:16:17) in.
38 (39:41:43) cm

width
33½ (36:38:40½) in.
85 (91:97:103) cm

BOLERO

BACK

Using larger hook, ch 49 (53:57:61).

Foundation row 1 sc into 2nd ch from hook, 1 sc in each ch to end, turn. 48 (52:56:60) sts.

Row 1 (WS) Ch 2 (counts as 1 hdc), 1 hdc in each st ending 1 hdc in tch, turn.

Row 2 Ch 1 (counts as 1 sc), 1 sc in each st, ending 1 sc in tch, turn.

These 2 rows form the patt and are repeated throughout.

Cont in patt, inc 1 st at each end of the next and 2 foll 4th rows. 54 (58:62:66) sts.

Cont straight until work measures 6¼ in. (16 cm) from beg, ending with a WS row.

Shape armholes

Next row Ss across and into the 6th st, ch 1 (counts as 1 sc), 1 sc in each st to last 5 sts, turn.
44 (48:52:56) sts.

Work 1 row straight.

Next row Ch 1 (counts as 1 sc), sc2tog, 1 sc in each st to last 3 sts, sc2tog, 1 sc in tch, turn.

Rep the last 2 rows, 1 (2:3:4) more times.
40 (42:44:46) sts.

Work 1 row, ending with a WS row. Fasten off.

LEFT FRONT

Using larger hook, ch 25 (27:29:31).

Foundation row As given for Back. 24 (26:28:30) sts.

Cont in patt as given for Back inc 1 st at end of the 3rd and 2 foll 4th rows. 27 (29:31:33) sts.

Cont straight until Left Front measures the same as Back to armhole, ending with a WS row.

Shape armhole

Next row Ss across and into the 6th st, ch 1 (counts as 1 sc), 1 sc in each st, ending 1 sc in tch, turn.
22 (24:26:28) sts. Work 1 row.

Dec 1 st at armhole edge on the next and 1 (2:3:4) foll alt rows. 20 (21:22:23) sts. Work 1 row, ending with a WS row.

Fasten off.

RIGHT FRONT

Using larger hook, ch 25 (27:29:31).

Foundation row As given for Back. 24 (26:28:30) sts.

Cont in patt as given for Back, inc 1 st at beg of 3rd and 2 foll 4th rows, 27 (29:31:33) sts.

Cont straight until Right Front measures the same as the Back to armhole, ending with a WS row.

Shape armhole

Next row Ch 1 (counts as 1 sc), 1 sc in each st to last 5 sts, turn. 22 (24:26:28) sts.

Work 1 row straight.

Dec 1 st at armhole edge on the next and 1 (2:3:4) foll alt rows. 20 (21:22:23) sts. Work 1 row, ending with a WS row. Fasten off.

SLEEVES (make 2)

Using larger hook, ch 35 (37:39:41).

Foundation row As given for Back. 34 (36:38:40) sts. Cont in patt as given for Back, inc 1 st at each end of the 6 foll alt rows. 46 (48:50:52) sts. Cont straight until sleeve measures 6¼ in. (16 cm) from beg, ending with a WS row.

Shape armholes

Next row Ss across and into the 6th st, ch 1 (counts as 1 sc), 1 sc in each st to last 5 sts, turn. 36 (38:40:42) sts.

Work 1 row straight.

Dec 1 st at each end of the next and 1 (2:3:4) foll alt rows. 32 sts. Work 1 row, ending with a WS row.

Fasten off.

YOKE

Join armhole seams, then join side and sleeve seams. With RS facing and using larger hook, rejoin yarn to Right Front.

Next row Ch 1 (counts as 1 sc), 1 sc in each of rem 19 (20:21:22) sts, work 32 sc along top of right sleeve, 40 (42:44:46) sc along back, 32 sc along left sleeve, 20 (21:22:23) sc along left front.
144 (148:152:156) sts.

Work 3 rows straight.

Dec row 1 Ch 1 (counts as 1 sc), 1 sc in each of next 3 (5:2:4) sts, *sc2tog, 1 sc in each of next 7 sts; rep from * 14 (14:15:15) times, sc2tog, 1 sc in each of next 2 (4:2:4) sts, 1 sc in tch, turn. 128 (132:135:139) sts.

Work 3 rows straight.

Dec row 2 Ch 1 (counts as 1 sc), 1 sc in each of next 3 (5:2:4) sts, *sc2tog, 1 sc in each of next 6 sts; rep from * 14 (14:15:15) times, sc2tog, 1 sc in each of next 1 (3:1:3) sts, 1 sc in tch, turn. 112 (116:118:122) sts.

Work 3 rows straight.

Dec row 3 Ch 1 (counts as 1 sc), 1 sc in each of next 2 (4:1:3) sts, *sc2tog, 1 sc in each of next 5 sts; rep from * 14 (14:15:15) times, sc2tog, 1 sc in each of next 2 (4:2:4) sts. 96 (100:101:105) sts.

Work 5 rows straight.

Dec row 4 Ch 1 (counts as 1 sc), 1 sc in each of next 1 (3:1:3) sts, *sc2tog, 1 sc in each of next 3 sts; rep from * 17 (17:18:18) times, sc2tog, 1 sc in each of next 2 (4:2:4) sts. 77 (81:81:85) sts.

Work 3 rows straight.

Dec row 5 Ch 1 (counts as 1 sc), 1 sc in next st, *sc2tog, 1 sc in next st; rep from * 23 (24:24:25) times, sc2tog, 1 sc in next 1 (2:2:3) sts, turn. 52 (55:55:58) sts.

Work 1 row straight. Fasten off.

FRONT EDGE

With RS facing and using smaller hook, rejoin yarn at lower edge of Right Front, ch 1 (counts as 1 sc), work in sc evenly around Right Front, neck, and Left Front, working 2 sc into each corner on neck.

Work 2 more rows in sc. Do not turn.

Next row With RS facing, work 1 row of crab st (sc worked from left to right instead of right to left) around front edge.

FINISHING

Fasten off

Weave in all yarn ends.

The yoke is formed by working across all the pieces.

Simple Chic

This shrug is worked in one piece from cuff to cuff in an unusual textured stitch. Flattering for any occasion, this may be a garment you'll want to make in several different colors.

Skill level: INTERMEDIATE

MEASUREMENTS

To fit bust

32–34	36–38	40–42	in.
81–86	91–97	102–107	cm

Length from cuff to cuff

57	60	62	in.
145	152	158	cm

Sleeve seam

17½ in. (44 cm)

MATERIALS

- 4 (5:6) × 140 g (5 oz.) balls of Lion Cotton in Seaspray 123

- E/4 (3.50 mm) and G/6 (4.25 mm) crochet hooks

GAUGE

14 sc to 4 in. (10 cm) and the 6 pattern rows to 2½ in. (6 cm) using G/6 (4.25 mm) crochet hook. Change hook size, if necessary, to obtain this gauge.

ABBREVIATIONS

tr2tog—leaving last loop of each st on hook, work 1 tr into each of the next 2 sts, yoh and draw through rem 3 loops on hook to dec 1 st.
sc2tog—as tr2tog, but work sc instead of tr.
See also page 11.

NOTES

Figures in parentheses refer to the larger sizes; where only one set of figures is given, this refers to all sizes. The shrug is worked in one piece from cuff to cuff.

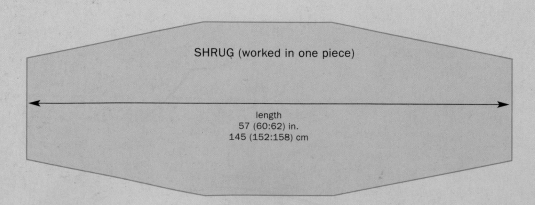

SHRUG (worked in one piece)

length
57 (60:62) in.
145 (152:158) cm

Basic shape of flat piece before sleeve edges are sewn together.

SHRUG

Using larger hook, ch 33 (37:41).

Foundation row (RS) 1 sc into 2nd ch from hook, 1 sc in each ch to end, turn. 32 (36:40) sts.

Rows 1–3 Ch 1 (counts as 1 sc), 1 sc in each st ending 1 sc in tch, turn.

Row 4 Ch 4 (counts as 1 tr), 1 tr in next sc, *skip 3 sc, 1 tr into next sc, 1 tr into each of 3 sc skipped, working *behind* last tr; rep from * to last 2 sc, 1 tr into each sc, turn.

Row 5 Ch 4 (counts as 1 tr), 1 tr into next tr, *skip 3 tr, 1 tr into next tr, 1 tr into each of 3 tr skipped, working *in front of* last tr; rep from * to last 2 tr, 1 tr into tr, 1 tr into top of tch, turn.

Row 6 Ch 1 (counts as 1 sc), 1 sc into each st ending 1 sc in tch, turn.

These 6 rows form the zigzag patt and are repeated throughout.

Cont in patt:

Rows 7 and 9 (inc) Ch 1 (counts as 1 sc), 1 sc at base of 1 ch, 1 sc in each st to last st, 2 sc in last st, turn.

Row 10 (inc) Ch 4 (counts as 1 tr), 1 tr at base of 4 ch, patt to last st, 2 tr in last st, turn.

Row 11 Ch 4 (counts as 1 tr), *skip 3 tr, 1 tr into next tr, 1 tr into each of 3 tr skipped, working *in front of* last tr; rep from * to last st, 1 tr in tch, turn.

Row 12 As Row 6.

Row 13 As Row 6.

Row 14 Ch 1 (counts as 1 sc), 1 sc at base of 1 ch, 1 sc in each st to last st, 2 sc in last st, turn.

Row 15 As Row 6.

Row 16 Ch 4 (counts as 1 tr), 1 tr at base of 4 ch, patt to last st, 2 tr in last st, turn.

Row 17 Ch 4 (counts as 1 tr), 1 tr in each of the next 2 tr, *skip 3 tr, 1 tr into next tr, 1 tr into each of 3 tr skipped working in front of last tr; rep from * to last 3 tr, 1 tr in each st, turn.

Row 18 As Row 6.

Row 19 As Row 6.

Row 20 As Row 14.

Row 21 As Row 6.

Rep Rows 10–21 two more times.

60 (64:68) sts.

Place a marker at each end of last row for ends of sleeves. A total of 46 rows, including Foundation Row, have been worked.

BACK

Inc 1 st at each end of Row 1, cont straight in patt for another 56 (62:68) rows, dec 1 st at each end of last row, thus ending with Row 5 of zigzag patt. Place a marker at each end of last row for beginning of sleeves.

2nd SLEEVE

Working in reverse order, work Rows 21–10 twice, then Rows 21–1, but dec 1 st at each end of every row where there was an inc 1 st at each end previously, as follows:

Row 21 As Row 6.

Row 20 Ch 1 (counts as 1 sc), sc2tog, 1 sc in each st to the last 3 sts, sc2tog, 1 sc in tch, turn.

Row 19 As Row 6.

Row 18 As Row 6.

Row 17 Ch 4 (counts as 1 tr), 1 tr in each of the next 2 sts; *skip 3 sc, 1 tr into next sc, 1 tr into each of 3 sc skipped, working *behind* last tr; rep from * to last 3 sts, 1 tr in each of the next 2 sc, 1 tr in tch, turn.

Cont as now set until 2nd sleeve matches 1st sleeve to lower edge, ending with 4 rows sc. Fasten off.

FINISHING

Join sleeves to markers.

Weave in yarn ends.

Edging

With RS facing and using smaller hook, rejoin yarn at top of one sleeve seam, ch 1 (counts as 1 sc), work in sc evenly around body edges, ss to 1 ch at beg, turn. Work 1 more row in sc. Fasten off. Weave in yarn ends.

Sunny Summer Stripes

This eye-catching sleeveless top is worked in a soft cotton yarn in bright, cheery colors. The front and back pieces are worked in the same way. A perfect summer top that looks great with the Retro Tote on page 97.

Skill level: INTERMEDIATE

MEASUREMENTS

To fit bust

32	34	36	38	in.
81	86	91	97	cm

Actual width

31½	33½	35½	38	in.
80	85	90	96	cm

Length from shoulder

20½	20½	21	21¼	in.
52	52	53	54	cm

MATERIALS

- 2 (2:3:3) × 50 g (1¾ oz.) balls of Rowan Handknit Cotton DK in Flame 254 (A)

- 3 (3:4:5) × 50 g (1¾ oz.) balls of Rowan Handknit Cotton DK in Mango Fool (319) (B)

- 2 (2:3:3) × 50 g (1¾ oz.) balls of Rowan Handknit Cotton DK in Ecru 251 (C)

- E/4 (3.50 mm) and G/6 (4.25 mm) crochet hooks

GAUGE

15 dc and 8 rows to 4 in. (10 cm) measured over double crochet pattern using G/6 (4.25 mm) crochet hook. Change hook size, if necessary, to obtain this gauge.

ABBREVIATIONS

dc2tog—leaving last loop of each st on hook, work 1 dc into each of next 2 sts, yoh, and draw through all 3 loops, to dec 1 st.
See also page 11.

NOTE

Figures in parentheses refer to the larger sizes; where only one set of figures is given, this refers to all sizes.

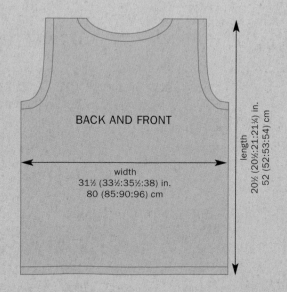

BACK AND FRONT

width
31½ (33½:35½:38) in.
80 (85:90:96) cm

length
20½ (20½:21:21¼) in.
52 (52:53:54) cm

TOP

BACK AND FRONT (both alike)

Using larger hook and A, ch 62 (66:70:74).

Foundation row (RS) 1 dc into 4th ch from hook, 1 dc into each ch to end, turn. 60 (64:68:72) sts. Fasten off yarn at end of every row—use end of yarn to join that row of side seam.

Row 1 Using C, ch 3 (counts as 1 dc) 1 dc into each dc, 1 dc into top of 3 ch, turn.

Row 2 Using B, work as Row 1.

Row 3 Using A, work as Row 1.

These 3 rows form patt. Cont in patt until work measures 11½ in. (29 cm) from beg.

Shape armholes

Next row Rejoin yarn to the 6th (6th:7th:8th) st, ch 3 (counts as 1 dc), 1 dc into each dc to last 5 (5:6:7) sts, turn. 50 (54:56:58) sts.

Next row Ch 3 (counts as 1 dc), 1 dc into each dc, 1 dc into top of 3 ch, turn.

Next row Ch 3 (counts as 1 dc), dc2tog, 1 dc into each dc to last 3 sts, dc2tog, 1 dc into top of 3 ch, turn.

Rep the last 2 rows 2 more times. 44 (48:50:52) sts.

Patt straight until armholes measure 6 (6:6¼:6¾) in. (15 [15:16:17] cm) from beg of shaping.

Shape neck

Next row Ch 3 (counts as 1 dc), work 1 dc into each of the next 9 (11:11:11) dc, turn. Work on these sts for the first side.

Dec 1 st at neck edge on next 3 rows. 7 (9:9:9) sts.

Patt 1 row. Fasten off.

Leave the center 24 (24:26:28) sts, rejoin yarn to next dc, ch 3 (counts as 1 dc), 1 dc into each dc, 1 dc into top of 3 ch, turn. Complete to match first side.

FINISHING

Neckband

Join shoulders.

With RS facing and using smaller hook, rejoin B at one shoulder seam, ch 1 (counts as 1 sc), work in sc evenly around neck edge, ss to 1 ch, turn.

Next round Ch 1 (counts as 1 sc), 1 sc into each sc to end, ss to 1 ch, turn.

Work 2 more rounds in sc. Fasten off.

Armbands

Join side seams.

With RS facing and using smaller hook, rejoin B at top of side seam, ch 1 (counts as 1 sc), work in sc evenly around armhole edge, ss to 1 ch, turn.

Next round Ch 1 (counts as 1 sc), 1 sc in each sc to end, ss to 1 ch, turn.

Work 2 more rounds in sc. Fasten off. Weave in yarn ends.

Lower edge

With RS facing and using smaller hook, rejoin B at one side seam, ch 1 (counts as 1 sc), work in sc evenly around lower edge, ss to 1 ch, turn.

Next round Ch 1 (counts as 1 sc), 1 sc in each sc to end, ss to 1 ch, turn.

Work 2 more rounds in sc. Fasten off. Weave in yarn ends.

See page 97 for the matching Retro Tote.

Little Red-Hooded Poncho

This gorgeous one-size-fits-all poncho, worked in brightly-colored yarns, is great for keeping warm on cool days. It is an easy-to-work garment with minimal shaping that is a good choice for a first crochet project.

Skill level: BEGINNER

MEASUREMENTS

One size
Actual width (front section only)
38½ in. (98 cm)

Length from shoulder
27 in. (68 cm)

MATERIALS

- 16 × 70 g (2½ oz.) balls of Lion Bouclé in Popsicle 212 (A)

- 3 × 140 g (5 oz.) balls of Lion Cotton in Poppy Red 112 (B)

- L/11 (8 mm) crochet hook

GAUGE

7½ hdc and 7 rows to 4 in. (10 cm) measured over pattern, using L/11 (8.00 mm) crochet hook and A. Change hook size, if necessary, to obtain this gauge.

ABBREVIATIONS

hdc3tog—[yoh, insert hook into next sp, yoh and draw loop through] 3 times, yoh and draw through all 7 loops. *See also page 11.*

NOTE

Use color B double throughout.

PONCHO

BACK AND FRONT (worked in one piece)

Beg with Back.
Using A, ch 71.
Row 1 (RS) With A, 1 hdc into 3rd ch from hook, 1 hdc in each ch to end. 70 sts.
Row 2 With A, ch 2 (counts as 1 hdc), 1 hdc into next sp (between stems [see Triple crochet, page 17] and below all horizontal threads connecting sts) and each sp to end, turn. 70 sts.

Row 2 forms patt and is repeated throughout.
Rep Row 2, 10 more times.
Change to B (used double) and patt 4 rows. Change to A and patt 12 rows.
Rep last 16 rows once more.
Change to B and patt 4 rows.

Shape neck

Row 1 With A, ch 2 (counts as 1 hdc), 1 hdc into next 27 sps, turn and work on these 28 sts for first side.
Patt 2 rows in A.
Row 4 With A, ch 2 (counts as 1 hdc), 1 hdc into first st (inc worked), patt to end.
Row 5 With A, patt to last sp, 2 hdc in last sp (inc worked).
Row 6 As Row 4. 31 sts.
Row 7 With A, patt to end then ch 5.
Row 8 With A, 1 hdc into 3rd ch from hook, 1 hdc into each of next 2 ch, 1 hdc into each sp to end. 35 sts.
Patt 4 more rows A.
Change to B and patt 2 rows. Fasten off.

Work 2nd side thus:

Row 1 With RS facing, leave center 14 sts for back neck, rejoin A to next st, ch 2 (counts as 1hdc), 1hdc in each sp to end, turn. 28 sts.

Patt 2 rows A.

Row 4 With A, patt to last sp, 2 hdc into last sp (inc worked).

Row 5 With A, ch 2, 1 hdc into first st (inc worked), patt to end.

Row 6 As Row 4. 31 sts.

Patt 1 row.

Join a short length of A to top of 2 ch at beg of last row, ch 4 and fasten off this short length of A.

Row 8 Patt to end, 1 hdc into each of 4 ch. 35 sts.

Patt 4 more rows in A.

Change to B and patt 2 rows. Fasten off.

With RS facing, rejoin B to first side and patt 2 rows across all 70 sts.

Patt 12 rows A, 4 rows B, and 12 rows A. Fasten off.

HOOD (make 2)

Using A, ch 6.

Row 1 (RS) 1 hdc into 3rd ch from hook, 1 hdc in each ch to end. 5 sts.

Row 2 Ch 2 (counts as 1 hdc), 1 hdc in each sp to end, ch 6, turn.

Row 3 1 hdc into 3rd ch from hook, 1 hdc into each of next 3 ch, 1 hdc in each sp to end, turn.

Rep last 2 rows 2 more times. 20 sts.

Patt 13 rows.

Shape top

Row 1 Hdc3tog, patt to end.

Row 2 Patt to last 3 sts, hdc3tog, turn.

Rep last 2 rows once more. 12 sts. Fasten off.

FINISHING

Sew top and back seam on hood, then sew lower edge of hood to neck edge. Weave in all yarn ends.

Edging

With RS facing, join B (used double) to one corner of poncho, ch 1, then work in sc evenly around outer edge, working 2 sc into each corner, ss to first ch, turn.

Next round Ch 1 (counts as 1 sc), 1 sc in each sc working 2 sc into each corner, ss to first ch. Fasten off. Weave in yarn ends.

Hood and opening edge

With RS facing, join B (used double) to base of front opening, ch 1, then work a row of sc evenly up first side of opening, around hood, and down 2nd side of opening, turn.

Next row Ch 1 (count as 1 sc), 1 sc in each sc to end. Fasten off. Weave in yarn ends.

Overlap ends at base of opening and sew in place. Weave in yarn ends.

Ties (make 2)

With B (used double), ch 30. Fasten off. Weave in yarn ends.

Sew one tie to top of opening at each side of neck.

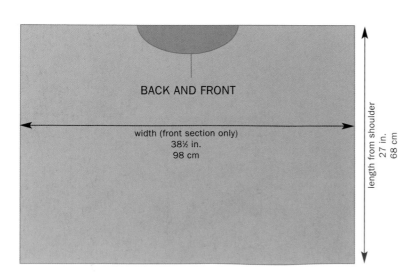

BACK AND FRONT

width (front section only)
38½ in.
98 cm

length from shoulder
27 in.
68 cm

SIDE OF HOOD

Tie-Front Bolero

Worked in a 4-ply cotton yarn, this easy bolero is made up of motifs that can be worked separately and sewn together at the end (or attached to each other as each motif is completed). You'll be amazed at how quickly you finish this garment!

 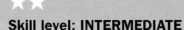

Skill level: INTERMEDIATE

MEASUREMENTS

To fit bust

30–32	34–38	in.
76–81	86–97	cm

Actual width

31½	39½	in.
80	100	cm

Length from shoulder

13¼	16	in.
33.5	41	cm

Sleeve seam

16	18	in.
41	46	cm

MATERIALS

• 9 (10) × 50 g (1¾ oz.) balls of Rowan 4-ply Cotton in Aegean 129

• C/2 (2.75 mm) crochet hook

GAUGE

One square measures 2 × 2 in. (5 × 5 cm) using C/2 (2.75 mm) crochet hook. Change hook size, if necessary, to obtain this gauge.

☐ square   —— right front
◺ triangle   ---- left front

ABBREVIATIONS

tr(3)4tog—leaving last loop of each st on hook, work 3 (4) triple crochet into stitch indicated, yoh, and pull through all loops on hook.
See also page 11.

NOTE

Figures in parentheses refer to the larger size; where only one set of figures is given this refers to both sizes.

larger size

 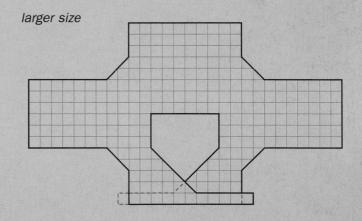

smaller size

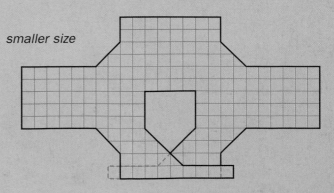

BOLERO

1st SQUARE

Ch 6, ss into first ch to form a ring.

Round 1 Ch 1, 16 sc into ring, ss in first sc.

Round 2 Ch 4, tr3tog into same st for first cluster, ch 3, skip next sc, [tr4tog, ch 3, skip next sc] 7 times, ss to top of first cluster. 8 petals.

Round 3 Ss into next 3-ch sp, ch 1, 1 sc in same sp, *ch 2, [3 hdc, ch 3, 3 hdc] into next 3-ch sp, ch 2, 1 sc in next 3-ch sp; rep from * 3 more times, omitting sc at end of last rep, ss to first sc. Fasten off.

2nd SQUARE

Work as First Square to end of Round 2.

Round 3 Ss into next 3-ch sp, ch 1, 1 sc into same sp, *ch 2, [3 hdc, ch 3, 3 hdc] into next 3-ch sp, ch 2, 1 sc into next 3-ch sp; rep from * once more, ch 2, 3 hdc into next 3-ch sp, ch 1, ss into corner 3-ch sp on First Square, ch 1, 3 hdc into same 3-ch sp on 2nd Square, ch 2, 1 sc in next 3-ch sp on 2nd Square and ss into corresponding sc on First Square, ch 2, 3 hdc into next 3-ch sp, ch 1, ss into corner 3-ch sp on First Square, ch 1, 3 hdc into same 3-ch sp on 2nd Square, ch 2, ss to first sc. Fasten off.

TRIANGLE

Ch 6, ss into first ch to form a ring.

Row 1 Ch 1, work 10 sc into ring, turn.

Row 2 Ch 6 (for first tr and 2-ch sp), skip first sc, [tr4tog into next sc, ch 3, skip next sc] 3 times, tr4tog into next sc, ch 2, skip next sc, 1 tr into last sc, turn.

Row 3 Ch 3, 3 hdc into first 2-ch sp, ch 2, 1 sc into next 3-ch sp, ch 2, [3 hdc, ch 3, 3 hdc] into next 3-ch sp, ch 2, 1 sc in next 3-ch sp, ch 2, (3 hdc, 1 tr) into last 2-ch sp. Fasten off.

Join half motifs on two sides to main motifs.

FINISHING

Make 180 (254) squares and 14 (16) triangles. Following chart, make and join a total of 180 (254) squares and 14 (16) triangles, joining on one or two sides as required. 4 (5) squares form ties on each front.

Edging

Join sleeve and side seams.

With RS facing, join yarn to right side seam.

Round 1 Ch 1, work sc evenly around entire outer edge, working 3 sc into each corner at ends of ties, ss to 1 ch, turn.

Round 2 Ch 1, 1 sc into each sc, working extra sts at outer corners and skipping 2 sts at inner corners, or as necessary, to keep edging flat, ss to 1 ch, turn.

Round 3 As Round 2.

Fasten off. Weave in yarn ends.

Cuffs (both alike)

With RS facing, join yarn at sleeve seam, ch 1, work sc evenly around sleeve, ss to 1 ch, turn.

Round 2 Ch 1, 1 sc into each sc, ss to 1 ch, turn.

Round 3 As Round 2.

Fasten off. Weave in yarn ends.

A simple edging in single crochet completes the bolero.

Go-Anywhere Vest

Vests like this one are so versatile, they can be worn alone or over a T-shirt or blouse. Worked in a super-soft cotton yarn, these border squares provide a unique look but are simple to crochet.

★★

Skill level: INTERMEDIATE

MEASUREMENTS

To fit bust

32–34	36–38	40–42	in.
81–86	91–97	102–107	cm

Actual width

36	40	44	in.
91	101	111	cm

Length from shoulder

23	24	25	in.
58	61	64	cm

MATERIALS

- 7 (8:9) × 50 g (1¾ oz.) balls of Rowan RYC Cashsoft Baby DK in Horseradish 801 (A)

- 1 × 50 g (1¾ oz.) ball of Rowan RYC Cashcotton DK in Geranium 604 (B)

- 1 × 50 g (1¾ oz.) ball of Rowan RYC Cashsoft Baby DK in Imp 803 (C)

- E/4 (3.50 mm) and G/6 (4.25 mm) crochet hooks

- 7 buttons, ½ in. (12 mm) in diameter

GAUGE

One motif measures 4 × 4 in. (10 × 10 cm), using G/6 (4.25 mm) crochet hook.

14 sts and 12 rows to 4 in. (10 cm) measured over pattern using G/6 (4.25 mm) crochet hook. Change hook sizes, if necessary, to obtain this gauge.

ABBREVIATIONS

tr2tog—work 2 tr into space until 1 loop of each remains on hook, yoh and through all 3 loops on hook.
dc2tog—as tr2tog, but work dc instead of tr.
cluster—work 3 dc into space until 1 loop of each remains on hook, yoh and through all 4 loops on hook.
See also page 11.

NOTE

Figures in parentheses refer to larger sizes; where only one set of figures is given, this refers to all sizes.

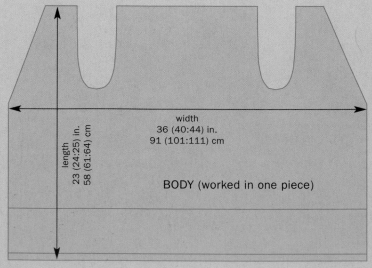

length
23 (24:25) in.
58 (61:64) cm

width
36 (40:44) in.
91 (101:111) cm

BODY (worked in one piece)

VEST

MOTIF SQUARES

Using larger hook, ch 10, ss into first ch to form a ring.

Round 1 Ch 4, 1 tr into ring, ch 2, into ring work [tr2tog, ch 2] 11 times, ss into first tr.

Round 2 Ss into 2-ch sp, ch 3 (counts as 1 dc), into same 2-ch sp as ss work 2 dc until 1 loop of each remains on hook, yoh and through all 3 loops on hook (for first cluster), ch 3, [1 cluster into next 2-ch sp, ch 3] 11 times, ss into top of first cluster.

Round 3 Ch 5 (counts as 1 hdc and 3 ch), skip first 3-ch arch, into next 3-ch arch work [1 cluster, ch 2, 1 cluster, ch 4, 1 cluster, ch 2, 1 cluster], ch 3, *skip next 3-ch arch, 1 hdc into top of next cluster, ch 3, skip next 3-ch arch, into next 3-ch arch work [1 cluster, ch 2, 1 cluster, ch 4, 1 cluster, ch 2, 1 cluster], ch 3; rep from * twice more, ss into 2nd of 5 ch at beg of round.

Round 4 Ch 1, work 1 sc into same st as last ss, *3 sc into next 3-ch sp, 1 sc into next cluster, 2 sc into next 2-ch sp, 1 sc into next cluster, 5 sc into next 4-ch arch, 1 sc into next cluster, 2 sc into next 2-ch sp, 1 sc into next cluster, 3 sc into next 3-ch sp, 1 sc into next hdc; ** rep from * 3 more times omitting 1 sc at end of last rep, ss into first sc. Fasten off.

HALF MOTIF (only used for 2nd size)

Ch 10 ch, ss into first ch to form a ring.

Row 1 Ch 4, 1 tr into ring, into ring work [ch 2, tr2tog] 5 times, turn.

Row 2 Ch 5 (counts as 1 dc and 2 ch), [1 cluster into next 2-ch sp, ch 3] 5 times, end last rep ch 2, 1 dc into top of tch, turn.

Row 3 Ch 5 (counts as 1 hdc and 3 ch), skip first cluster, into next 3-ch arch work [1 cluster, ch 2, 1 cluster, ch 4, 1 cluster, ch 2, 1 cluster], ch 3, skip next 3-ch arch, 1 hdc into top of next cluster, ch 3, skip next 3-ch arch, into next 3-ch arch work [1 cluster, ch 2, 1 cluster, ch 4, 1 cluster, ch 2, 1 cluster], ch 3, 1 hdc into 3rd of 5 ch at beg of previous row, turn.

Row 4 Ch 1 (counts as 1 sc), *3 sc into first 3-ch sp, 1 sc into top of next cluster, 2 sc into next 2-ch sp, 1 sc into next cluster, 5 sc into next 4-ch arch, 1 sc into next cluster, 2 sc into next 2-ch sp, 1 sc into next cluster, 3 sc into next 3-ch sp, 1 sc into next hdc; rep from *

once more, working last sc into 4th of 5 ch at beg of last row. Fasten off.

MOTIF BORDER

1st and 3rd sizes only

Work first motif in B.

Work 2nd motif in C until Round 3 is complete.

Round 4 Work to **, rep from * once more, 3 sc into next 3-ch sp, 1 sc into next cluster, 2 sc into next 2-ch sp, 1 sc into next cluster, 3 sc into next 4-ch arch, ss to same st on first motif, 2 sc into same 4-ch arch, 1 sc into next cluster, ss to same st on first motif, 2 sc into next 2-ch sp, 1 sc into next cluster, ss to same st on first motif, 3 sc into next 3-ch sp, 1 sc into next hdc, ss to same st on first motif, 3 sc into next 3-ch sp, 1 sc into next cluster, ss to same st on first motif, 2 sc into next 2-ch sp, 1 sc into next cluster, ss to same st on first motif, 3 sc into next 4-ch arch, ss to same st on first motif, 2 sc into same 4-ch sp, 1 sc into top of next cluster, 2 sc into next 2-ch sp, 1 sc into top of next cluster, 3 sc into next 3-ch sp, ss into first sc. Fasten off.

Work and join 7 (9) more motifs, alternating colors B and C, ending strip with motif in B.

2nd size only

Work half motif in B.

Work 2nd motif in C until Round 3 is complete.

Round 4 As given for first and 3rd sizes.

Work and join 8 more motifs, alternating colors B and C, ending strip with half motif in B.

BODY (worked in one piece to armholes)

With RS facing and using larger hook, join A to corner of first motif.

1st and 3rd sizes only

Next row Ch 1 (counts as 1 sc), work 13 more sc along top of first motif, 14 sc along each remaining motif.

2nd size only

Next row Ch 1 (counts as 1 sc), work 6 more sc along first half motif, 14 sc along each full motif ending 7 sc along last half motif.

All sizes

Work 1 more row in sc.

Next row Ch 3 (counts as 1 dc), 1 dc into each sc, ending 1 dc in tch, turn.

Cont in patt as follows:

Row 1 Ch 3 (counts as 1 dc), *work 1 dc into next sp (between stems of these sts [see page 17] and below all horizontal threads connecting sts), 1 dc into each sp to end, turn. 126 (140:154) sts.

This row forms the patt and is repeated throughout.

Cont until work measures 9¾ (10¼:10½) in. (25 [26:27] cm) from beg of dc patt, ending with a WS row.

Front slope

Next row Ch 3 (counts as 1 dc), dc2tog, patt to last 3 sts, dc2tog, 1 dc in last sp, turn.

Work 1 row.

Rep the last 2 rows once more. 122 (136:150) sts.

RIGHT FRONT

Next row Ch 3 (counts as 1 dc), dc2tog, patt another 22 (24:27) sts, turn. Work on these 24 (26:29) sts for right front.

Work 6 (7:7) rows, dec 1 st at armhole edge on every row and cont to dec 1 st at front slope on every alt row. 15 (16:19) sts.

Keeping armhole edge straight, cont to dec 1 st at front edge on next (next:2nd) row and every foll alt row until 10 (11:12) sts rem. Cont straight until armhole measures 7½ (8¼:9) in. (19 [21:23] cm) from beg of shaping, ending at armhole edge.

Shape shoulder

Next row Ss across and into the 6th (6th:7th) st, ch 3 (counts as 1 dc), patt to end. 5 (6:6) sts. Fasten off.

BACK

With RS facing, leave 8 (10:12) sts for armhole, rejoin A to next st, ch 3 (counts as 1 dc), 1 dc into each of next 55 (61:65) sps, turn.

Cont on these 56 (62:66) sts for back.

Work 6 (7:7) rows, dec 1 st at each end of every row. 44 (48:52) sts.

Cont straight until back measures same as front to beg of shoulder shaping.

Shape shoulders

Next row Ss across and into the 6th (6th:7th) st, ch 3 (counts as 1 dc), patt to last 5 (5:6) sts. Fasten off.

Mark the center 24 (26:28) sts for back neck.

LEFT FRONT

With RS facing, leave 8 (10:12) sts for armhole, rejoin A to next st, ch 3 (counts as 1 dc), patt to last 3 sts, dc2tog, 1 dc into last sp, turn. 24 (26:29) sts. Work to match Right Front to shoulder, but end at front edge.

Shape shoulder

Next row Patt to last 5 (5:6) sts. Fasten off.

FINISHING

Join shoulders. Weave in yarn ends.

Lower edging

With RS facing and using smaller hook, join C to top corner of square or half motif on Left Front. Ch 1 (counts as 1 sc), work in sc evenly along side of first motif, 2 sc into corner, then in sc along entire lower edge, 2 sc into corner, then in sc up side of last motif to top corner of motif, turn.

Work 1 more row in sc, working 2 sc in each corner. Fasten off. Weave in yarn ends.

Front edging

With RS facing and using smaller hook, join A to first row in sc above motif border on right front, ch 1 (counts as 1 sc), ss to lower edging, work in sc evenly around front edge to same point above motifs on left front, ss to lower edging, turn.

Mark the positions of 7 buttons, the first ½ in. (1 cm) up from motif and the last ½ in. (1 cm) down from Row 1 worked for front slope, with the remainder spaced evenly between.

Work 1 more row in sc, ss to lower edging at each end and making buttonholes to correspond with markers for buttons as follows: ch 2, skip 2 sc. Fasten off. Weave in yarn ends.

Armbands (both alike)

With RS facing and using smaller hook, join A at center of armhole, ch 1 (counts as 1 sc), work in sc evenly around armhole edge, ss to 1 ch at beg, turn.

Work 1 more round in sc. Fasten off. Sew on buttons.

Wraparound Jacket

This wraparound cardigan can be worn for many different occasions; pair it with your favorite jeans for a casual look, wear it over a turtleneck with a long skirt, or use it as a topper with a dress for evening.

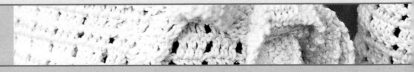

Skill level: ADVANCED

MEASUREMENTS

To fit bust

32–34	36–38	40–42	in.
81–86	91–97	102–107	cm

Actual width

34½	40	43¼	in.
87	101	110	cm

Length from shoulder

23	23½	24½	in.
58	60	62	cm

Sleeve seam

17½	18	18½	in.
45	46	47	cm

MATERIALS

- 8 (9:10) × 100 g (3½ oz.) balls of Sirdar Cotton DK in Cream 021

- E/4 (3.50 mm) crochet hook

GAUGE

18 sts and 9 rows to 4 in. (10 cm) measured over pattern using E/4 (3.50 mm) crochet hook. Change hook size, if necessary, to obtain this gauge.

ABBREVIATIONS

dc2(3)tog—leaving last loop of each st on hook, work 1 dc into each of next 2 (3) sts, yoh and draw through rem 3 (4) loops on hook, to dec 1 (2) sts.
See also page 11.

NOTES

Figures in parentheses refer to the larger sizes; where only one set of figures is given, this refers to all sizes. When decreasing over filet patt (1dc, ch 1, skip next st, 1dc into next st), work a dc into ch sp to work dc3tog.

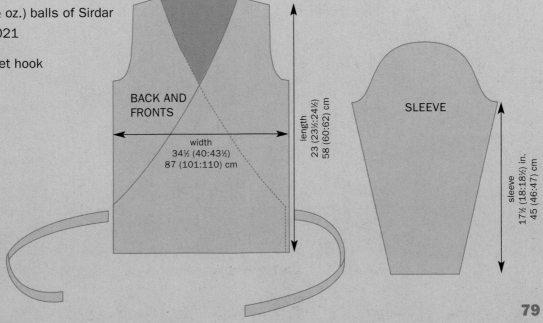

BACK AND FRONTS

width
34½ (40:43½)
87 (101:110) cm

length
23 (23½:24½) in.
58 (60:62) cm

SLEEVE

sleeve
17½ (18:18½) in.
45 (46:47) cm

TOP

BACK

Ch 80 (92:100).

Foundation row 1 sc into 3rd ch from hook, 1 sc into each ch to end, turn, 79 (91:99) sts.

Row 1 Ch 1 (counts as first sc), 1 sc into each st to end, turn.

Rows 2 and 3 As Row 1. Cont in patt:

Next row (RS) Ch 3 (counts as first dc), 1 dc into each of next 2 sts, *ch 1, skip next st, 1 dc into each of next 3 sts, rep from * to end, turn.

Rep the last row throughout. **

Work another 31 rows.

Shape armholes

Next row Ss into each of the first 6 (8:9) sts, ch 3, patt to last 5 (7:8) sts, turn. 69 (77:83) sts.

Next row Dc2tog, patt to last 2 sts, dc2tog.

Rep last row 1 (2:3) more times. 65 (71:75) sts.

Work straight for another 15 (16:17) rows.

Shape shoulders

Next row Ss into each of first 10 (11:12) sts, ch 3, patt to 9 (10:11) sts, turn.

Next row Ss into each of first 11 (12:13) sts, ch 3, patt to last 10 (11:12) sts.

Fasten off. 27 (29:29) sts.

LEFT FRONT

Work as given for Back to **. 79 (91:99) sts.

Work another 12 rows.

Shape front

Row 1 (WS) Dc3tog, patt to end, turn.

Row 2 Patt to last 3 sts, dc3tog, turn, 75 (87:95) sts.

Rep Rows 1 and 2 eight more times, then work Row 1 again. 41 (53:61) sts.

Shape armhole

Next row Ss into each of first 6 (8:9) sts, ch 3, patt to last 3 sts, dc3tog, turn. 34 (44:51) sts.

Next row Dc3tog, patt to last 2 sts, dc2tog, turn. 31 (41:48) sts.

1st size only

Next row Dc2tog, patt to last 2 sts, dc2tog, turn. 29 sts. Keeping armhole edge straight, cont to dec 1 st at front edge on next 10 rows. 19 sts.

2nd and 3rd sizes only

Next row Dc2tog, patt to last 3 sts, dc3tog, turn. 38 (45) sts.

Next row Dc3tog, patt to last 2 sts, dc2tog, turn. 35 (42) sts.

Next row Dc0(2)tog, patt to last 3 sts, dc3tog, turn. 33 (39) sts.

Keeping armhole edge straight, cont to dec 2 (2) sts at front edge on next 3 (7) rows. 27 (25) sts. Dec 1 st at front edge on next 6 (2) rows.

All sizes

19 (21:23) sts. Work 5 (6:8) rows straight.

Shape shoulder

Next row Ss into each of first 10 (11:12) sts, patt to end. Fasten off. 10 (11:12) sts.

RIGHT FRONT

Work as given for Left Front—the patt is reversible.

SLEEVES (make 2)

Ch 48 (52:56).

Foundation row 1 sc into 3rd ch from hook, 1 sc into each ch to end, turn. 47 (51:55) sts.

left and right: A simple tie completes the jacket.

Rows 1–3 As given for Back.

Cont in patt as Back, inc 1 st at each end of 3rd and every foll 4th row until there are 65 (69:73) sts, working inc sts into patt. Patt straight until Sleeve measures 17½ (18:18½) in. (45 [46:47] cm).

Shape top

Next row Ss into each of first 6 (8:9) sts, patt to last 5 (7:8) sts, turn. 55 (55:57) sts.

Next row Dc3tog, patt to last 3 sts, dc3tog. 51 (51:53) sts.

Rep the last row 9 (8:8) more times. 15 (19:21) sts.

2nd and 3rd sizes only

Next row Dc2tog, patt to last 2 sts, dc2tog, turn.

Rep last row 2 (3) times. 13 sts.

All sizes

Fasten off. Weave in yarn ends.

FRONT EDGING

Join shoulder seams.

With RS facing , join yarn at hem edge on Right Front.

Row 1 Ch 1, work in sc evenly around front edges to hem edge on Left Front, working a multiple of 2 sts plus 1, turn.

Row 2 Ch 1 (counts as 1 sc), 1 sc in each st to end, turn.

Row 3 Ch 1 (counts as 1 sc), *ch 3, skip next st, 1 sc into next st; rep from * to end. Fasten off. Weave in yarn ends.

TIES

Ch 5.

Next row 1 sc into 2nd ch from hook, 1 sc in each of 3 ch, turn. 4 sts.

Next row Ch 1 (counts as 1 sc), 1 sc in each st to end, turn.

Rep the last row until tie measures approximately 16 in. (40 cm). Fasten off. This will be the right tie. For the left tie, work as given above until tie measures approximately 32 in. (81 cm).

FINISHING

Sew ties to fronts, under edging, and level with last 2 rows below front shaping. Set in sleeves. Join side seams, leaving 2 rows open on right side seam in line with ties for tie to go through. Join sleeve seams.

ACCESSORIES

Scarves, shawls, hats, and bags—must-have accessories that are perfect for a weekend project because they are all simple and quick to make. From a fashionable hip-hugging belt to a stylish tote, you'll find a wonderful range of items in a range of textures and colors.

Tote Bag with Motif Border

Quick and easy to create, this tote, worked in a soft cotton yarn of bright summery colors, would make an ideal carryall for shopping trips or for holding your favorite crochet projects. And the motifs are fast and fun to crochet, as well as fashionable.

★
Skill level: BEGINNER

MEASUREMENTS

12 × 12 in. (31 × 31 cm)

MATERIALS

- 1 × 50 g (1¾ oz.) ball of Rowan RYC Cashsoft Baby DK in Imp 803 (A)

- 1 × 50 g (1¾ oz.) ball of Rowan RYC Cashcotton DK in Geranium 604 (B)

- 1 × 50 g (1¾ oz.) ball of Rowan RYC Cashcotton DK in Pool 602 (C)

- E/4 (3.50 mm) and G/6 (4.25 mm) crochet hook

- ⅜ yd. (40 cm) lining, ¾ yd. (75 cm) wide

- Matching sewing thread and sewing needle

GAUGE

One motif measures 4 × 4 in. (10 × 10 cm) using G/6 (4.25 mm) crochet hook.
4 sts and 12 rows to 4 in. (10 cm) measured over pattern, using G/6 (4.25 mm) crochet hook. Change hook sizes, if necessary, to obtain this gauge.

ABBREVIATIONS

tr2tog—work 2 tr into space until 1 loop of each remains on hook, yoh and through all 3 loops on hook.
cluster—work 3 dc into space until 1 loop of each remains on hook, yoh and through all 4 loops on hook.
See also page 11.

BAG

MOTIF SQUARES

Using larger hook and appropriate color, ch 10, ss into first ch to form a ring.
Round 1 Ch 4, 1 tr into ring, ch 2, into ring work [tr2tog, ch 2] 11 times, ss into first tr.
Round 2 Ss into 2-ch sp, ch 3 (counts as 1 dc), into same 2-ch sp as ss work 2 dc until 1 loop of each remains on hook, yoh and through all 3 loops on hook (for first cluster), ch 3, [1 cluster into next 2-ch sp, ch 3] 11 times, ss into top of first cluster.
Round 3 Ch 5 (counts as 1 hdc and 3 ch), skip first 3-ch arch, into next 3 ch-arch work [1 cluster, ch 2, 1 cluster, ch 4, 1 cluster, ch 2, 1 cluster], ch 3, *skip next 3-ch arch, 1 hdc into top of next cluster, ch 3, skip next 3-ch arch, into next 3-ch arch work [1 cluster, ch 2, 1 cluster, ch 4, 1 cluster, ch 2, 1 cluster], ch 3; rep from * twice more, ss into 2nd of 5 ch at beg of round.
Round 4 Ch 1, work 1 sc into same st as last ss, *3 sc into next 3-ch sp, 1 sc into next cluster, 2 sc into next 2-ch sp, 1 sc into next cluster, 5 sc into next 4-ch arch, 1 sc into next cluster, 2 sc into next 2-ch sp, 1 sc into next cluster, 3 sc into next 3-ch sp, 1 sc into next hdc; ** rep from * 3 more times omitting 1 sc at end of last rep, ss into first sc.

   Fasten off.

MOTIF BORDER

1st side

Work first motif in A.

Work 2nd motif in B until Round 3 is complete.

Round 4 Work to **, rep from * once more, 3 sc into next 3-ch sp, 1 sc into next cluster, 2 sc into next 2-ch sp, 1 sc into next cluster, 3 sc into next 4-ch arch, ss to same st on first motif, 2 sc into same 4-ch arch, 1 sc into next cluster, ss to same st on first motif, 2 sc into next 2-ch sp, 1 sc into next cluster, ss to same st on first motif, 3 sc into next 3-ch sp, 1 sc into next hdc, ss to same st on first motif, 3 sc into next 3-ch sp, 1 sc into next cluster, ss to same st on first motif, 2 sc into next 2-ch sp, 1 sc into next cluster, ss to same st on first motif, 3 sc into next 4-ch arch, ss to same st on first motif, 2 sc into same 4-ch sp, 1 sc into top of next cluster, 2 sc into next 2-ch sp, 1 sc into top of next cluster, 3 sc into next 3-ch sp, ss into first sc. Fasten off. Work 3rd motif in C joining to 2nd motif.

2nd side

Work 4th motif in A joining to 3rd motif.

Work 5th motif in B joining to 4th motif.

Work 6th motif in C, joining to 5th and first motifs.

MAIN BODY

With RS facing and using larger hook, join A to corner of first motif in A, ch 1 (counts as 1 sc), work 15 more sc along top edge of first motif, 16 sc along top edge of every foll motif, ss to 1 ch at beg, turn. 96 sts.

Round 1 Using A, ch 3 (counts as 1 dc), *work 1 dc into next sp (between stems of sts [see Triple crochet, page 17] and below all horizontal threads connecting sts), 1 dc into each sp to end, ss to top of 3 ch, turn.

Rounds 2 and 3 Using C work as Round 1.

Rounds 4 and 5 Using B work as Round 1.

Round 6 Using A, work as Round 1.

These 6 rounds form the patt.

Rep these 6 rounds 2 more times, then Rounds 1, 2, and 3 again.

Shape for handles

Using smaller hook and B, proceed as follows:

Round 1 Ch 1, 1 sc into each st to end, ss to 1 ch at beg, turn.

Round 2 Ch 1, 1 sc into each of next 13 sc, ch 20, skip 20 sc, 1 sc into each of next 28 sc, ch 20, skip 20 sc, 1 sc into each of next 14 sc, ss to 1 ch at beg, turn.

Round 3 Ch 1, 1 sc into each of next 12 sc, skip 1 sc, 1 sc into each of next 20 ch, skip 1 sc, 1 sc into each of next 26 sc, skip 1 sc, 1 sc into each of next 20 ch, skip 1 sc, 1 sc into each of next 13 sc, ss to 1 ch at beg, turn.

Round 4 Ch 1, 1 sc into each of next 12 sc, skip 1 sc, 1 sc into each of next 18 sc, skip 1 sc, 1 sc into each of next 26 sc, skip 1 sc, 1 sc into each of next 18 sc, skip 1 sc, 1 sc into each of next 13 sc, ss to 1 ch at beg, turn.

Rounds 5–7 Ch 1, 1 sc into each sc to end, ss to 1 ch at beg, turn.

Round 8 Skip 1 sc, *3 sc in next sc, skip 1 sc, rep from * to last sc, 3 sc in next sc, ss to first sc. Fasten off.

BASE

Using smaller hook and A, ch 102, ss to first ch to form a ring.

Round 1 Ch 1 (counts as 1 sc), 2 sc into ch on which 1 ch stands, 1 sc into each of next 50 ch, 3 sc into next ch, 1 sc into each of next 50 ch, ss to 1 ch. 106 sc.

Round 2 Ch 1, 3 sc into next sc, 1 sc into each of next 52 sc, 3 sc into next sc, 1 sc into each of next 51 sc, ss to 1 ch. 110 sc.

Work 3 rounds, working 3 sc in center sc at beg and center of round as before. 122 sc. Fasten off.

FINISHING

Join base seam with backstitch and matching yarn. Place center of shaped ends of base at side seam and opposite side edge, and join to motif border using backstitch and matching yarn.

Cut 2 pieces of lining material the same size as the bag plus ½ in. (1 cm) for a seam allowance all around. Join seams on 3 sides, then press ½ in. (1 cm) to WS along top edge of lining. Insert lining into bag. Using sewing thread and needle, sew top edge of lining neatly in place around first round worked for handles.

Weave in yarn ends.

Striped Scarf

This striking accessory, made in a soft cotton yarn, is worked in simple stripes using subtle colors, with motifs at each end. It can be worn with a coat for warmth or paired with jeans for added flair.

Skill level: BEGINNER

MEASUREMENTS

9½ × 59½ in. (24 × 151 cm)—excluding tassels

MATERIALS

- 2 × 50 g (1¾ oz.) balls of Sirdar Luxury Cotton DK in Vanilla Cream 653 (A)

- 2 × 50 g (1¾ oz.) balls of Sirdar Luxury Cotton DK in Walnut 656 (B)

- 2 × 50 g (1¾ oz.) balls of Sirdar Luxury Cotton DK in Sage 657 (C)

- G/6 (4.25 mm) crochet hook

GAUGE

15 sts and 8½ rows to 4 in. (10 cm) measured over dc patt using G/6 (4.25 mm) crochet hook. Motif measures 4¼ in. (11 cm) square, using G/6 (4.25 mm) crochet hook. Change hook size, if necessary, to obtain these gauges.

ABBREVIATIONS

tr2tog—work 2 tr into ring until 1 loop of each remains on hook, yoh and draw through all 3 loops on hook.
cluster—work 3 dc into sp until 1 loop of each remains on hook, yoh and draw through all 4 loops on hook.
See also page 11.

SCARF

FIRST MOTIF

Using A, ch 10, ss into first ch to form a ring.
Round 1 Using A, ch 4, 1 tr into ring, ch 2, into ring work [tr2tog, ch 2] 11 times, ss into first tr.
Round 2 Using A, ss into 2-ch sp, ch 3, into same 2-ch sp as ss work 2 dc until 1 loop of each remains on hook, yoh and through all 3 loops on hook (first cluster made), ch 3, [1 cluster into next 2-ch sp, ch 3] 11 times, ss into top of first cluster. Break off A.
Round 3 Join B to top of first cluster, ch 5 (count as 1 hdc, 3 ch), skip first 3-ch arch, into next 3-ch arch work [1 cluster, ch 2, 1 cluster, ch 4, 1 cluster, ch 2, 1 cluster], ch 3, *skip next 3-ch arch, 1 hdc into top of next cluster, ch 3, skip next 3-ch arch, into next 3-ch arch work [1 cluster, ch 2, 1 cluster, ch 4, 1 cluster, ch 2, 1 cluster], ch 3; rep from * twice more, ss into 2nd of 5 ch at beg of round.
Round 4 Using B, ch 1, work 1 sc into same st as last ss, *3 sc into next 3-ch sp, 1 sc into top of next cluster, 2 sc into next 2-ch sp, 1 sc into next cluster, 5 sc into next 4-ch arch, 1 sc into next cluster, 2 sc into next 2-ch sp, 1 sc into next cluster, 3 sc into next 3-ch sp, 1 sc into next hdc; rep from * 3 more times omitting 1 sc at end of last rep, ss into first sc. Fasten off.

SECOND MOTIF

Make a second motif working Rounds 1 and 2 in B and Round 3 in A.
Round 4 Using A, ch 1, work 1 sc into same st as last ss, *3 sc into next 3-ch sp, 1 sc into top of next cluster,

2 sc into next 2-ch sp, 1 sc into next cluster, 5 sc into next 4-ch arch, 1 sc into next cluster, 2 sc into next 2-ch sp, 1 sc into next cluster, 3 sc into next 3-ch sp, 1 sc into next hdc; rep from * once more, 3 sc into next 3-ch sp, 1 sc into top of next cluster, 2 sc into next 2-ch sp, 1 sc into next cluster, 3 sc into next 4-ch arch, ss to corresponding st on first motif, 2 sc into same 4-ch arch, 1 sc into next cluster, 2 sc into next 2-ch sp, 1 sc into next cluster and ss to corresponding st on first motif, 3 sc into next 3-ch arch, 1 sc into next hdc, ss to corresponding st on first motif, 3 sc into next 3-ch arch, 1 sc into next cluster, ss to corresponding st on first motif, 2 sc into next 2-ch sp, 1 sc into next cluster, 3 sc into next 4-ch arch, ss to corresponding st on first motif, 2 sc into same 4-ch arch, 1 sc into next cluster, 2 sc into next 2-ch sp, 1 sc into next cluster, 3 sc into next 3-ch sp, sl st into first sc.

Fasten off.

Work first and second motifs again for other end of scarf.

STRIPES

Using C and with RS facing, rejoin yarn to corner of first motif.

Row 1 Using C, ch 3 (counts as 1 dc), work 15 dc along first motif, 1 dc into ss between motifs and 16 dc along second motif, turn. 33sts.

Row 2 Using A, ch 3 (counts as 1 dc), work 1 dc in each st, ending 1 dc in top of 3 ch, turn.

Row 3 Using B, ch 3 (counts as 1 dc), work 1 dc in each st, ending 1 dc in top of 3 ch, turn.

These 3 rows form the patt. Rep these 3 rows 35 more times.

Next row Using C, ch 3 (counts as first dc) ss to corner of first motif, work another 15 dc, joining each to a sc of 1st motif with a ss, 1 dc and ss to ss between motifs, work another 16 dc and ss along 2nd motif.

Fasten off.

FINISHING

Edging

Round 1 Using C and with RS facing, rejoin yarn to corner of first motif and work ch 1 (counts as first sc), *work another 31 sc along edges of first and 2nd motifs, 3 sc into corner, then work in sc evenly along long edge of scarf, 3 sc into corner, rep from * once, ending 2 sc into corner, ss to 1 ch at beg of round, turn.

Round 2 Ch 1 (counts as 1 sc), 1 sc in each sc and 3 sc into center sc at each corner, ss to 1 ch.

Fasten off.

Tassels

For each tassel cut 6 lengths of yarn each 10 in. (25 cm) long. Fold in half and knot tassels, evenly spaced, along each end of scarf as desired. You could make the tassels all in one color or in all three colors, as in the photograph. Trim the ends of the tassels, if necessary.

Make the tassels in all three colors, or just one if you prefer.

Openwork Hip Hugger

You'll love wearing this belt with a sweater or a pair of jeans for an up-to-date fashion accessory. You can add beads to the ties, or sew sequins at intervals along the belt for a more glamorous look.

★★
Skill level: INTERMEDIATE

MEASUREMENTS

2¾ in. (7 cm) x desired length

MATERIALS

- 1 × 100 g (3½ oz.) ball of Sirdar Breeze DK in Buttermilk 063

- C/2 (2.75 mm) crochet hook

- 6 wooden beads, ¼ in. (5 mm) in diameter with large hole

GAUGE

Center portion of belt measures 1¾ in. (4.5 cm) wide, and 14 rows measure 4 in. (10 cm) using C/2 (2.75 mm) crochet hook. Change hook size, if necessary, to obtain this gauge.

ABBREVIATIONS

See page 11.

BELT

CENTER PORTION

Ch 16.

Row 1 1 sc into 12th ch from hook, 1 sc into each of the next 4 ch, turn.

Row 2 Ch 7 (counts as 1 dc and 4 ch), skip 5 sc, 5 sc into next ch arch, turn.

Row 3 Ch 7 (counts as 1 dc and 4 ch), skip 5 sc, 4 sc into next ch arch, 1 sc in 3rd of 7 ch at beg of last row, turn.

Row 3 forms the patt. Cont in patt until Center Portion of belt is desired length. Fasten off.

SIDES

Rejoin yarn to right-hand corner of one long edge.

Row 1 Ch 1, (count as 1 sc), work in sc evenly along long edge so that there is a multiple of 2 sts, 2 sc into corner, 8 sc along short edge, 2 sc into corner, then work same number of sc along other long edge, work 2 sc into corner, work 8 sc along short edge, 1 sc into same place as 1 ch at beg of round, ss to 1 ch at beg.

Row 2 Ch 2 (counts as 1 hdc), 1 hdc into same st, *ch 1, skip next st, 1 hdc into next st; rep from * along long edge, working last hdc in the 2nd of the 2 sc at corner, 1 hdc into same st as last hdc (for corner)**, along short edge work (ch 1, skip next st, 1 hdc into next st) 5 times, 1 hdc into same st as last hdc, rep from * to ** once, along short edge work (ch 1, skip next st, 1 hdc into next st) 4 times, ch 1, skip next st, ss to top of 2 ch.

Row 3 Ch 1 (counts as 1 sc), 1 sc in each st, ss to 1 ch at beg of round. Fasten off. Weave in yarn ends.

TIES—both ends alike

Cut 3 lengths of yarn approximately 34 in. (86 cm) long, fold in half, and draw loop through center of one end of belt. Draw ends of strands through loop and tighten.

Using 2 strands tog, braid to within 3 in. (8 cm) of ends of yarn. Attach one bead to each 2-strand length and knot ends to secure bead. Rep at other end of belt.

Ruffled Boa

Create a clever spiraling scarf combining beautiful yarns to keep you both warm and stylish on even the coldest winter day. Use neutral shades, as shown here, to complement a casual daytime look, or choose classic black to top an evening outfit.

Skill level: BEGINNER

MEASUREMENTS

Actual size

3 × 59 in. (8 × 150 cm)

MATERIALS

- 6 × 50 g (1¾ oz.) balls of Sirdar Funky Fur in Latte 550 (A)

- 2 × 100 g (3½ oz.) balls of Sirdar Wash 'n' Wear Crepe 4 ply in Beige 283 (B)

- G/6 (4.25 mm) crochet hook

GAUGE

First 5 rows measure 2 in. (5 cm) using G/6 (4.25 mm) hook. Change hook size, if necessary, to obtain this gauge.

ABBREVIATIONS

See page 11.

SCARF

Using B, make a chain 59 in. (150 cm) long.

Row 1 1 sc into 2nd ch from hook, 1 sc into each ch to end, turn.

Join in A.

Row 2 Using A, ch 3 (counts as first dc), 1 dc into sc at base of 3 ch, 2 dc into each sc to end, turn.

Row 3 Using A, ch 3 (counts as first dc), 1 dc into dc at base of 3 ch, 2 dc into each dc to end, working last 2 dc into top of 3 ch at beg of previous row, turn.

Row 4 Using B, ch 3 (counts as first dc), 1 dc into dc at base of 3 ch, 2 dc into each dc to end, working last 2 dc into top of 3 ch at beg of previous row, turn.

Row 5 As Row 3.

Break off A and cont using B only.

Row 6 Ch 1 (does NOT count as st), *2 sc into next dc, 1 sc into next dc, rep from * to end, working last sc into top of 3 ch at beg of previous row, turn.

Row 7 Ch 1 (does NOT count as st), *1 sc into next 2 sc, ch 3, 1 sc into top of last sc, 2 sc into next sc, rep from * to end.

Fasten off. Weave in yarn ends.

FINISHING

Weave in yarn ends.

The boa should not be pressed.

Luxurious Shawl

This shawl, created with an elegant silky-looking yarn, will steal the show. Worked in simple motifs with a lacy edging and fringing, this wrap is perfect for cool summer evenings.

MEASUREMENTS

71 × 34¼ in. (180 × 87 cm)

MATERIALS

- 13 × 50 g (1¾ oz.) balls of Sirdar Silky Look DK in Pewter 978

- G/6 (4.25 mm) crochet hook

GAUGE

One square = 4 × 4 in. (10 x 10 cm) using G/6 (4.25 mm) crochet hook. Change hook size if necessary to obtain this gauge.

ABBREVIATIONS

dc2(3)tog—leaving last loop of each st on hook, work 1 dc into each of the next 2 (3) sts, yoh and draw through all 3 (4) loops on hook to dec 1 st.
See also page 11.

FIRST SQUARE MOTIF

Ch 6 and join with a ss to form a ring.
Round 1 Ch 3, dc2tog into ring (counts as dc3tog, called cluster), [ch 3, dc3tog into ring] 7 times, ch 3, ss to top of first cluster.
Round 2 Ss to center of next 3-ch arch, ch 1, 1 sc into same place, [ch 5, 1 sc into next arch] 7 times, ch 2, 1 dc into first sc.
Round 3 *Ch 5, [dc3tog, ch 3, dc3tog] into next arch **, ch 5, 1 sc into next arch; rep from * two more times and from * to ** again, ch 2, 1 dc into dc that closed Round 2.
Round 4 * Ch 5, 1 sc into next arch, ch 5, [1 sc, ch 5, 1 sc] into corner 3-ch arch, ch 5, 1 sc into next 5-ch arch; rep from * 3 times, ending last rep with 2 ch, 1 dc into dc that closed Round 3, ss to first ch.
Round 5 Ch 1, 2 sc into sp under dc, 5 sc in each 5-ch sp and 1 sc in each sc, ending 3 sc into same sp as first 2 sc, ss to first sc.
   Fasten off.

SECOND SQUARE MOTIF

Work Rounds 1–4 as given for First Motif.
Round 5 Ch 1, 1 sc into same place, 2 sc into same ch arch, [1 sc into next sc, 5 sc into next 5-ch arch] twice, *1 sc into next sc, 5 sc into corner 5-ch arch, [1 sc into next sc, 5 sc into next 5-ch arch] 3 times; rep from * once more, [1 sc into next sc, 3 sc into next 5-ch arch, ss to corresponding st on first motif, 2 sc into same ch arch] 5 times in all, 1 sc into next sc, 2 sc into same 5-ch arch as first 3 sc, ss to first sc.
   Fasten off.

Continue joining each subsequent motif in this way. Work a total of 64 square motifs and 16 triangle motifs, joining each motif to the next in rows as shown in diagram.

TRIANGLE MOTIF

Ch 6 and join with a ss to form a ring.
Row 1 Ch 3, dc2tog into ring (counts as dc3tog, called cluster), [ch 3, dc3tog into ring] 4 times, turn.
Row 2 [ch 5, 1 sc into next arch] 4 times, ch 2, 1 dc in top of next cluster, turn.
Row 3 Ch 3, dc2tog into st at base of 3 ch, ch 5, 1 sc into next arch, ch 5, [dc3tog, ch 3, dc3tog] into next arch, ch 5, 1 sc into next arch, ch 5, dc3tog into 3rd of 5 ch at beg of last row, turn.
Row 4 Ch 5, 1 sc at base of 5 ch, [ch 5, 1 sc into next 5-ch arch] twice, ch 5, [1 sc, ch 5, 1 sc] into corner 3-ch arch, [ch 5, 1 sc into next 5-ch arch] twice, ch 5, 1 sc into top of next cluster, ch 2, 1 dc into same cluster, turn.
Row 5 Ch 1, 1 sc in same space as 1 ch, 2 sc in same arch, complete to match Round 5 of square motif, joining 2nd side to end of square motif, 2 sc in last ch sp, 1 sc into 3rd of 5 ch at beg of last row. Fasten off.

TOP EDGING

With RS facing, rejoin yarn to right-hand corner of top edge, ch 1 (counts as 1 sc) work in sc evenly along the top edge of shawl, turn.

Next row Ch 1 (counts as 1 sc), work 1 sc in each sc to end, 1 sc in 1 ch at beg, turn.

Work 2 more rows in sc. Fasten off.

SIDE EDGING

With RS facing, rejoin yarn to top left-hand corner of shawl and work along edge of shawl as follows:
Row 1 Ch 1, work 177 sc evenly along first side of shawl, 15 sc evenly along bottom square, and 177 sc evenly along second side. 369 sts, turn.
Row 2 Ch 4 (counts as 1 dc and 1 ch), skip first 2 sc, *1 dc in next dc, ch 1, skip next dc; rep from * ending 1 dc in tch, turn.
Row 3 Ch 1, 1 sc into first dc, *ch 5, skip 1 ch, 1 dc, ch 1, 1 sc into next dc; rep from * ending 1 sc into 3rd of 4 ch, turn.
Row 4 Ch 1, 1 sc into first sc, work 7 sc into each 5-ch arch to end, 1 sc into last sc, turn.
Row 5 Ch 5 (counts as 1 dc and 2 ch), skip first 4 sc, 1 sc into next sc, *ch 3, skip 6 sc, 1 sc into next sc; rep from * to last 4 sc, ch 2, 1 dc into last sc, turn.
Row 6 Ch 1, 1 sc into first dc, ch 2, 1 sc into 2-ch sp, into each sp work [1 sc, ch 5, 1 sc] to end, ending 1 sc in last sp, ch 2, 1 sc in 3rd of 5 ch at beg of previous row. Fasten off.

FINISHING

Make the fringe. For each tassel cut 6 strands of yarn approx. 15 in. (38 cm) long. Fold strands in half, then knot strands to every other arch.

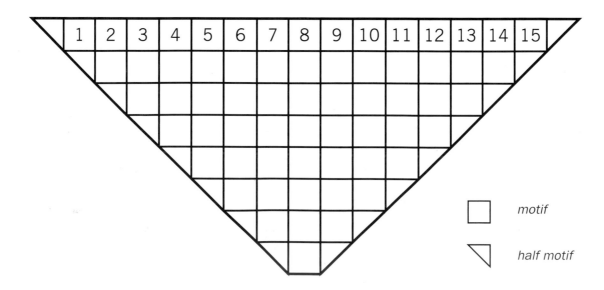

1	2	3	4	5	6	7	8	9	10	11	12	13	14	15

☐ motif

◺ half motif

Retro Tote

This generously sized bag is worked in bright colors and is a variation on traditional granny squares. It can be created with either a long or short strap to fit your lifestyle. Wear this bag with the sleeveless top on page 65 for an eye-catching set.

Skill level: BEGINNER

MEASUREMENTS

Actual size
9½ × 10¼ in. (24 × 26 cm)

MATERIALS

- 2 × 50 g (1¾ oz.) balls of Rowan Handknit Cotton in Flame 254 (A)

- 1 × 50 g (1¾ oz.) ball of Rowan Handknit Cotton in Mango Fool 319 (B)

- 1 × 50 g (1¾ oz.) ball of Rowan Handknit Cotton in Ecru 251 (C)

- G/6 (4.25 mm) crochet hook

- ⅜ yd. (30 cm) lining material

- Matching sewing thread and sewing needle

GAUGE

One motif measures 4¾ × 4¾ in. (12 × 12 cm) using size G/6 (4.25 mm) crochet hook. Change hook size, if necessary, to obtain this gauge.

ABBREVIATIONS

See page 11.

BAG

BACK AND FRONT (both alike)

1st motif
Using A, ch 6, join with a ss to form a ring.
Round 1 Ch 1, 16 sc into ring, ss to first sc. 16 sts.
Round 2 Ch 6 (count as 1 dc and 3-ch arch), skip next st, [1 dc into next st, ch 3, skip next st] 7 times, ss to 3rd of 6 ch.
Round 3 Ch 1, work a petal of [1 sc, 1 hdc, 5 dc, 1 hdc, 1 sc] into each 3-ch arch, ss to first sc. Fasten off.
Round 4 Join B to first dc of any petal of Round 3, ch 1, 1 sc into same place as 1 ch, ch 4, skip 3 dc, 1 sc into next dc, [ch 4, 1 sc into first dc of next petal, ch 4, skip 3 dc, 1 sc into next dc] 7 times, ch 2, 1 hdc into first sc.
Round 5 Ch 3 (counts as 1 dc), 2 dc into arch formed by hdc that closed Round 4, *ch 1, 1 sc into next arch, [ch 3, 1 sc into next arch] twice, ch 1, ** [3 dc, ch 3, 3 dc] into next arch; rep from * twice, then from * to ** again, ending [3 dc, ch 3] into last ch arch, ss to top of 3 ch. Fasten off.

2nd motif
Work Rounds 1, 2, and 3 in B and Round 4 in A as given for 1st Motif.
Round 5 Using A, ch 3 (counts as 1 dc), 2 dc into arch formed by hdc that closed 4th round, *ch 1, 1 sc into next arch, [ch 3, 1 sc into next arch] twice, ch 1 ** [3 dc, ch 3, 3 dc] into next arch; rep from * once, ch 1, 1 sc into next arch, [ch 3, 1 sc into next arch] twice, ch 1, [3 dc, ch 1, ss to corner arch on 1st Motif, ch 1,

2 dc, ss to same dc on 1st Motif, 1 dc] into next arch, ch 1, 1 sc into next arch, ss to same sc on 1st Motif, [ch 3, 1 sc into next arch, ss to same sc on 1st Motif] twice, ch 1, 1 dc, ss to same dc on 1st Motif, 2 dc, ch 1, ss to corner on 1st Motif, ch 1, ss to top of 3 ch. Fasten off.

3rd motif

Work Rounds 1, 2, and 3 in C and work Rounds 4 and 5 in A, joining to 1st Motif on Round 5 as before.
　　Fasten off.

4th motif

Work Rounds 1, 2, and 3 in B with Rounds 4 and 5 in C, joining to 2nd and 3rd motifs on Round 5.
　　Fasten off.

TOP

With RS facing, join B to top corner, ch 1, work in sc evenly along top edge, turn.
　　Work 9 more rows in sc. Fasten off. Fold in half to WS and slipstitch in place. Repeat for second side.
　　Weave in all yarn ends.

GUSSET AND STRAP

Using A, ch 7.

Next row Ch 1 into 2nd ch from hook, 1 sc into each ch to end, turn. 6 sts.

　　Work in sc until piece is long enough to fit from center of lower edge of motifs, along base, up the side, to desired length for strap, then down rem side and base. Sew to three sides on back and front pieces, then join base seam, using a crocheted ss. Weave in yarn ends.

FINISHING

Cut lining fabric the same size as the bag to under the top edge, adding ½ in. (1 cm) seam allowance all around.
　　Join sides and base of lining pieces. Fold seam allowance at top to wrong side; baste. Insert lining into bag and, using sewing thread, slipstitch in place around top, just under top edging.

This bag and the sleeveless top on page 65 make a fashionable duo.

Creamy Cloche

Just the thing for sunny days, this stylish hat is worked in a simple lace pattern with the crown and brim in single crochet. Keep it in your pocket or handbag and pull it out whenever the weather turns cool!

Skill level: INTERMEDIATE

MEASUREMENTS

To fit width around head (approx.)
20½ (22) in.
52 (56) cm

MATERIALS

- 2 × 100 g (3½ oz.) balls of Sirdar Cotton DK in Cream 023

- E/4 (3.50 mm) and G/6 (4.25 mm) crochet hooks

GAUGE

18 stitches and 20 rows to 4 in. (10 cm) measured over sc using G/6 (4.25 mm) hook. Change hook size, if necessary, to obtain this gauge.

ABBREVIATIONS

See page 11.

NOTE

Figures in parentheses refer to the larger size; where only one set of figures is given, this refers to both sizes.

HAT

Using smaller hook, ch 5, join with a ss to form a ring.
Round 1 (RS) Ch 1, (counts as 1 sc), 7 sc into ring, join with ss to top of 1 ch. 8 sc.
Round 2 Ch 1, 1 sc into sc on which 1 ch stands, 2 sc into each sc to end, ss to top of 1 ch. 16 sc.
Round 3 Ch 1, 1 sc into sc on which 1 ch stands, 1 sc into next sc, *2 sc into next sc, 1 sc into next sc, rep from * to end, ss to top of 1 ch. 24 sc.
Round 4 Ch 1, 1 sc into sc on which 1 ch stands, 1 sc into each of next 2 sc, *2 sc into next sc, 1 sc into each of next 2 sc, rep from * to end, ss to top of 1 ch. 32 sc.
Round 5 Ch 1, 1 sc into sc on which 1 ch stands, 1 sc into each of next 3 sc, *2 sc into next sc, 1 sc into each of next 3 sc, rep from * to end, ss to top of 1 ch. 40 sc.
Round 6 Ch 1, 1 sc into sc on which 1 ch stands, 1 sc into each of next 4 sc, *2 sc into next sc, 1 sc into each of next 4 sc, rep from * to end, ss to top of 1 ch. 48 sc.
Round 7 Ch 1, 1 sc into each sc to end, ss to top of 1 ch.
Round 8 Ch 1, 1 sc into sc on which 1 ch stands, 1 sc into each of next 5 sc, *2 sc into next sc, 1 sc into each of next 5 sc, rep from * to end, ss to top of 1 ch. 56 sc.
Round 9 As Round 7.

Round 10 Ch 1, 1 sc into sc on which 1 ch stands, 1 sc into each of next 6 sc, *2 sc into next sc, 1 sc into each of next 6 sc, rep from * to end, ss to top of 1 ch. 64 sc.

Round 11 Ch 1, 1 sc into sc on which 1 sc stands, 1 sc into each of next 7 sc, *2 sc into next sc, 1 sc into each of next 7 sc, rep from * to end, ss to top of 1 ch. 72 sc.

Round 12 As Round 7.

Round 13 Ch 1, 1 sc into sc on which 1 ch stands, 1 sc into each of next 8 sc, *2 sc into next sc, 1 sc into each of next 8 sc, rep from * to end, ss to top of 1 ch. 80 sc.

Round 14 As Round 7.

1st size only

Round 15 Ch 1, 1 sc into sc on which 1 ch stands, 1 sc into each of next 19 sc, *2 sc into next sc, 1 sc into each of next 19 sc, rep from * to end, ss to top of 1 ch. 84 sc.

Round 16 Ch 1, 1 sc into sc on which 1 ch stands, 1 sc into each of next 11 sc, *2 sc into next sc, 1 sc into each of next 11 sc; rep from * to end, ss to top of 1 ch. 91 sc.

2nd size only

Round 15 Ch 1, 1 sc into sc on which 1 ch stands, 1 sc into each of next 9 sc, *2 sc into next sc, 1 sc into each of next 9 sc, rep from * to end, ss to top of 1 ch. 88 sc.

Round 16 As Round 7.

Round 17 Ch 1, 1 sc into sc on which 1 ch stands, 1 sc into each of next 10 sc, *2 sc into next sc, 1 sc into each of next 10 sc, rep from * to end, ss to top of 1 ch. 96 sc.

Round 18 As Round 7.

Round 19 Ch 1, 1 sc into sc on which 1 ch stands, 1 sc into each of next 47 sc, 2 sc in next sc, 1 sc in each sc to end, ss to top of 1 ch. 98 sc.

Round 20 As Round 7.

Both sizes

Change to larger hook and cont in patt as follows:

Round 1 Ch 3 (counts as 1 dc), 1 dc into next st, *skip 2 sts, into next st work (2 dc, ch 3, 2 dc), skip 2 sts, 1 dc into each of the next 2 sts; rep from * ending skip 2 sts, into next st work (2 dc, ch 3, 2 dc), skip 2 sts, ss to top of 3 ch at beg of round. 13 (14) patt repeats.

Round 2 Ch 3 (counts as 1 dc), 1 dc into next dc, * skip next 2 dc, into next 3-ch sp work (2 dc, ch 3, 2 dc), skip next 2 dc, 1 dc into each of next 2 dc; rep from * ending skip next 2 dc, (2 dc, 3 ch, 2 dc) into last 3-ch sp, ss to top of 3 ch at beg of round.

Rep Round 2 four (five) times.

Next round Ch 3 (counts as 1 dc), 1 dc into next dc, *ch 1, skip 2 dc, 3 sc into next 3-ch sp, ch 1, skip 2 dc, 1 dc into each of the next 2 dc; rep from * ending ch 1, skip 2 dc, 3 sc into next 3-ch sp, skip 2 dc, ch 1, ss to top of 3 ch at beg of round.

BRIM

Change to smaller hook.

Round 1 Ch 1 (counts as 1 sc), 1 sc into next dc, *1 sc into next ch, 1 sc into each of the next 3 sc, 1 sc into next ch, 1 sc into each of the next 2 dc; rep from * ending 1 sc into next ch, 1 sc into each of the next 3 sc, 1 sc into next ch, ss to 1 ch at beg of round. 91 (98) sc.

Round 2 Ch 1, 1 sc into each sc to end, ss to top of 1 ch, inc.

Round 3 Ch 1, 1 sc into sc on which 1 ch stands, *1 sc into each of next 5 (6) sc, 2 sc into next sc, rep from * to last 6 sc, 1 sc into next 6 sc, ss to top of 1 ch. 106 (112) sc.

Work 3 rounds straight.

Round 7 Ch 1, 1 sc into sc on which 1 ch stands, *1 sc into each of next 14 (15) sc, 2 sc into next sc, rep from * to last 15 sc, 1 sc into next 15 sc, ss to top of 1 ch, 113 (119) sc.

Work 3 rounds straight.

Round 11 Ch 1, 1 sc into sc on which 1 ch stands, *1 sc into each of next 10 (11) sc, 2 sc into next sc, rep from * to last 13 (10) sc, 1 sc into next 13 (10) sc, ss to top of 1 ch, 123 (129) sc.

Work 1 (2) rounds more straight.

Fasten off. Weave in yarn ends.

Skinny Scarf

Easy to crochet in just a few hours, this cute scarf is done in a shaggy yet warm and lightweight yarn on a really big crochet hook. Just combine simple chains and single crochet stitches worked into chain spaces.

★ **Skill level: BEGINNER**

MEASUREMENTS

Actual size
5½ × 79 in. (14 × 200 cm)

MATERIALS

- 2 × 50 g (1¾ oz.) balls of Sirdar Foxy in Silver Fox 434
- N/15 (10.00 mm) crochet hook

GAUGE

2 pattern repeats measure 4 in. (10 cm), and 4 rows measure 5 in. (13 cm) on N/15 (10.00 mm) hook. Change hook size, if necessary, to obtain this gauge.

ABBREVIATIONS

See page 11.

SCARF

Ch 16.
Row 1 1 sc into 8th ch from hook, ch 5, skip 3 ch, 1 sc into next ch, ch 5, skip 3 ch, 1 sc into last ch, turn.
Row 2 Ch 5, 1 sc into first ch sp, (ch 5, 1 sc into next ch sp) twice, turn. Rep last row until almost all yarn has been used up.
Next row Ch 4, 1 sc into first ch sp, (ch 3, 1 sc into next ch sp) twice.
   Fasten off.

FINISHING

Do not press the scarf.

This yarn creates a wonderful shaggy effect.

CHILDREN'S FASHIONS

Using the softest yarns in gorgeous colors, the projects in this chapter will be perfect for your little angels. The items use a range of different stitch patterns and techniques, helping you achieve wonderful results, from delicate lacy stitches to pretty ruffles and flower motifs. And since crochet is so versatile, it is also perfect for creating a zip-up cardigan or cozy sweater.

Mittens, Bootees, and Hat or Bonnet

Cozy toes, fingers, and heads are guaranteed with these beautiful baby items. Choose from the boy's set or the ruffled girl's coordinates—either way, they'll make a baby look adorable! Both are made in rounds of single crochet, so there are no seams to sew up.

Skill level: INTERMEDIATE

MEASUREMENTS

To fit age
0–3 months

Mitts, width around hand
4¼ in. (11 cm)

Bootees, length of foot
3½ in. (9 cm)

Hat, width around head
13¼ in. (34 cm)

Bonnet, width around face
13¼ in. (34 cm)

MATERIALS

Boy's set
- 2 × 50 g (1¾ oz.) balls of Sirdar Snuggly DK in Sky 216 (Mitts take approximately 15 g [½ oz.], Bootees approximately 20 g [⅔ oz.], and Hat approximately 20 g [⅔ oz.].)

- E/4 (3.50 mm) crochet hook

Girl's set
- 2 × 50 g (1¾ oz.) balls of Sirdar Snuggle DK in Blush Pink 202 (Mitts take approximately 20 g [⅔ oz.], Bootees approximately 30 g [1 oz.], and Bonnet approximately 40 g [1⅓ oz.].)

- E/4 (3.50 mm) crochet hook

GAUGE

19 stitches and 22 rows to 4 in. (10 cm) measured over single crochet fabric using E/4 (3.50 mm) hook. Change hook size, if necessary, to obtain this gauge.

ABBREVIATIONS

sc2tog—[insert hook as indicated in patt instructions, yoh, and draw loop through] twice, yoh, and draw through all 3 loops on hook.

sc3tog—[insert hook as indicated in patt instructions, yoh, and draw loop through] 3 times, yoh, and draw through all 4 loops on hook.

These abbreviations are specific to this pattern. See also page 11.

BOY'S COORDINATES

MITTENS (both alike)

Ch 5.

Round 1 (RS) 2 sc into 2nd ch from hook, 1 sc into each of next 2 ch, 4 sc into last ch, now working back along other side of foundation ch: 1 sc into each of next 2 ch, 2 sc into next ch—this is same ch as used for 2 sc at beg of round, ss to first sc, turn. 12 sts.

Round 2 Ch 1 (does not count as st), 2 sc into first sc, 1 sc into each of next 4 sc, 2 sc into each of next 2 sc, 1 sc into each of next 4 sc, 2 sc into last sc, ss to first sc, turn. 16 sts.

Round 3 Ch 1 (does not count as st), 2 sc into first sc, 1 sc into each of next 6 sc, 2 sc into each of next 2 sc, 1 sc into each of next 6 sc, 2 sc into last sc, ss to first sc, turn. 20 sts.

Round 4 Ch 1 (does not count as st), 1 sc into each sc to end, ss to first sc, turn.

Rounds 5–16 As Round 4.

Round 17 (RS) Ch 1 (does not count as st), 1 sc into first sc, *ch 1, skip 1 sc, 1 sc into next sc, rep from * to end, replacing sc at end of last rep with ss to first sc, turn.

Round 18 Ch 1 (does not count as st), 1 sc into first ch sp, (1 sc into next sc, 1 sc into next ch sp) 9 times, 1 sc into last sc, ss to first sc, turn.

Rounds 19–22 As Round 4, but do not turn at end of last round.

Now work 1 round of crab st (see page 21) into last round, ending with ss to first sc.

Fasten off. Weave in yarn ends.

Make tie

Using yarn double, ch 60, and fasten off. Weave in yarn ends. Thread Tie through ch sps of Round 17 and tie ends in a bow.

BOOTEES (both alike)

Ch 12.

Round 1 (RS) 1 sc into 2nd ch from hook, 1 sc into each of next 9 ch, 2 sc into last ch, now working back along other side of foundation ch: 1 sc into each of next 9 ch, 1 sc into last ch—this is same ch as used for sc at beg of round, ss to first sc, turn. 22 sts.

Round 2 Ch 1 (does not count as st), 2 sc into each of first 2 sc, 1 sc into each of next 7 sc, 2 sc into each of next 4 sc, 1 sc into each of next 7 sc, 2 sc into each of last 2 sc, ss to first sc, turn. 30 sts.

Round 3 Ch 1 (does not count as st), 1 sc into first sc, 2 sc into each of next 2 sc, 1 sc into each of next 9 sc, 2 sc into each of next 2 sc, 1 sc into each of next 2 sc, 2 sc into each of next 2 sc, 1 sc into each of next 9 sc, 2 sc into each of next 2 sc, 1 sc into last sc, ss to first sc, turn. 38 sts.

Round 4 Ch 1 (does not count as st), 1 sc into first sc, 2 sc into next sc, 1 sc into next sc, 2 sc into next sc, 1 sc into each of next 11 sc, 2 sc into next sc, 1 sc into next sc, 2 sc into next sc, 1 sc into each of next 2 sc, 2 sc into next sc, 1 sc into next sc, 2 sc into next sc, 1 sc into each of next 11 sc, (2 sc into next sc, 1 sc into next sc) twice, ss to first sc, turn. 46 sts.

Round 5 Ch 1 (does not count as st), 1 sc into each sc to end, ss to first sc, turn.

Rounds 6–10 As Round 5.

Shape instep

Row 1 Ch 1 (does not count as st), 1 sc into each of first 25 sc, sc3tog over next 3 sc, turn.

Row 2 Ch 1 (does not count as st), 1 sc into each of first 5 sts, sc3tog over next 3 sts, turn.

Row 3 Ch 1 (does not count as st), 1 sc into each of first 5 sts, sc3tog over next 3 sts—these are last st of instep and next 2 sts of Round 10, turn.

Row 4 Ch 1 (does not count as st), 1 sc into each of first 5 sts, sc3tog over next 3 sts—these are last st of instep and next 2 sts of Row 1, turn.

Rows 5–10 As Rows 3 and 4, 3 times.

Row 11 Ch 1 (does not count as st), 1 sc into each of first 6 sts, 1 sc into each of rem 10 sc of Round 10, ss to sc at beg of Row 1 of instep, turn.

Round 12 Ch 1 (does not count as st), 1 sc into each of first 9 sc, sc2tog over next 2 sts, 1 sc into each of next 4 sc, sc2tog over next 2 sts—this is last st of instep and next st of Row 1 of instep, 1 sc into each of next 9 sc, ss to first sc, turn. 24 sts.

Round 13 Ch 1 (does not count as st), 1 sc into first sc, *Ch 1, skip 1 sc, 1 sc into next sc, rep from * to end, replacing sc at end of last rep with ss to first sc, turn.

Round 14 Ch 1 (does not count as st), 1 sc into first ch sp, (1 sc into next sc, 1 sc into next ch sp) 11 times, 1 sc into last sc, ss to first sc, turn. 24 sts.

Round 15 Ch 1 (does not count as st), 1 sc into each sc to end, ss to first sc, turn.

Rounds 16–19 As Round 15, but do not turn at end of last round.

Now work 1 round of crab st (see page 21) into last round, ending with ss to first sc.

Fasten off. Weave in yarn ends.

Make tie

Using yarn double, ch 60, and fasten off. Weave in yarn ends. Thread Tie through ch sps of Round 13 and tie ends in a bow.

HAT

Ch 4 and join with a ss to form a ring.

Round 1 (RS) Ch 1 (does not count as st), 8 sc into ring, ss to first sc, turn.

Round 2 Ch 1 (does not count as st), 2 sc into each sc to end, ss to first sc, turn. 16 sts.

Round 3 Ch 1 (does not count as st), *1 sc into next sc, 2 sc into next sc, rep from * to end, ss to first sc, turn. 24 sts.

Round 4 Ch 1 (does not count as st), 1 sc into each sc to end, ss to first sc, turn.

Round 5 Ch 1 (does not count as st), *1 sc into each of next 2 sc, 2 sc into next sc, rep from * to end, ss to first sc, turn. 32 sts.

Round 6 As Round 4.

Round 7 Ch 1 (does not count as st), *1 sc into each of next 3 sc, 2 sc into next sc, rep from * to end, ss to first sc, turn. 40 sts.

Round 8 As Round 4.

Round 9 Ch 1 (does not count as st), *1 sc into each of next 4 sc, 2 sc into next sc, rep from * to end, ss to first sc, turn. 48 sts.

Round 10 As Round 4.

Round 11 Ch 1 (does not count as st), *1 sc into each of next 5 sc, 2 sc into next sc, rep from * to end, ss to first sc, turn. 56 sts.

Round 12 As Round 4.

Round 13 Ch 1 (does not count as st), *1 sc into each of next 6 sc, 2 sc into next sc, rep from * to end, ss to first sc, turn. 64 sts.

Rounds 14–29 As Round 4, but do not turn at end of last round.

Now work 1 round of crab st (see page 21) into last round, ending with ss to first sc.

Fasten off. Weave in yarn ends.

GIRL'S COORDINATES

MITTENS (both alike)

Work as given for Mittens of Boy's Set to end of Round 19.

Round 20 (WS) Ch 4 (counts as first dc and 1 ch), working into back loops only of round 19: 1 dc into first sc, ch 1, *(1 dc, ch 1, and 1 dc) into next sc, ch 1, rep from * to end, ss to 3rd of 4 ch at beg of round. Do not turn.

The added ruffles are so cute for a baby girl.

Round 21 Ss into first ch sp, *Ch 3, skip 1 dc, 1 ss into next ch sp, rep from * to end. Do not turn.

Round 22 Ss down 3 ch at beg of Round 20 and into front loop of sc of Round 19 used for first dc of Round 20, working into front loops only of Round 19: ch 1 (does not count as st), 1 sc into each sc to end, ss to first sc, turn.

Round 23 (RS) Ch 1 (does not count as st), 1 sc into each sc to end, ss to first sc, turn.

Round 24 (WS) Ch 4 (counts as first dc and 1 ch), 1 dc into first sc, ch 1, *(1 dc, ch 1, and 1 dc) into next sc, ch 1, rep from * to end, ss to 3rd of 4 ch at beg of round. Do not turn.

Round 25 As Round 21.

Fasten off.

Make tie

Using yarn double, ch 60, and fasten off. Weave in yarn ends.

Thread Tie through ch sps of Round 17 and tie ends in a bow.

BOOTEES (both alike)

Work as given for Bootees of Boy's Set to end of Round 15.

Round 16 (WS) Ch 4 (counts as first dc and 1 ch), working into back loops only of Round 15: 1 dc into first sc, ch 1, *(1 dc, ch 1, and 1 dc) into next sc, ch 1, rep from * to end, ss to 3rd of 4 ch at beg of round. Do not turn.

Round 17 Ss into first ch sp, *ch 3, skip 1 dc, 1 ss into next ch sp, rep from * to end. Do not turn.

Round 18 Ss down 3 ch at beg of round 16 and into front loop of sc of Round 15 used for first dc of round 16, working into front loops only of Round 15: ch 1 (does not count as st), 1 sc into each sc to end, ss to first sc, turn.

Round 19 (RS) Ch 1 (does not count as st), 1 sc into each sc to end, ss to first sc, turn.

Round 20 (WS) Ch 4 (counts as first dc and 1 ch), 1 dc into first sc, ch 1, *(1 dc, ch 1, and 1 dc) into next sc, ch 1, rep from * to end, ss to 3rd of 4 ch at beg of round. Do not turn.

Round 21 As Round 17.

Fasten off. Weave in yarn ends.

Make tie

Using yarn double, ch 60, and fasten off. Weave in yarn ends.

Thread Tie through ch sps of Round 13 and tie ends in a bow.

BONNET

Work as given for Hat of Boy's Set to end of Round 13.

Now working backward and forward in rows, not rounds, cont as follows:

Row 14 Ch 1 (does not count as st), 1 sc into each sc to end, turn.

Rows 15–27 As Row 14.

Row 28 (WS) Ch 4 (counts as first dc and 1 ch), working into back loops only of Row 27: 1 dc into first sc, *ch 1, (1 dc, ch 1, and 1 dc) into next sc, rep from * to end, turn.

Row 29 Ch 3, ss into first ch sp, *ch 3, skip 1 dc, 1 ss into next ch sp, rep from * until ss has been worked into last ch sp, ch 3, ss to 3rd of 4 ch at beg of previous row and down to base of this ch, turn.

Row 30 Working into front loops only of row 27: ch 1 (does not count as st), 1 sc into each sc to end, turn.

Row 31 Ch 1 (does not count as st), 1 sc into each sc to end, turn.

Row 32 (WS) Ch 4 (counts as first dc and 1 ch), 1 dc into first sc, *ch 1, (1 dc, ch 1, and 1 dc) into next sc, rep from * to end, turn.

Row 33 Ch 3, ss into first ch sp, *ch 3, skip 1 dc, 1 ss into next ch sp, rep from * until ss has been worked into last ch sp, ch 3, ss to 3rd of 4 ch at beg of previous row.

Fasten off. Weave in yarn ends.

Make neckband and ties

Ch 60 (for first tie). With RS facing and starting at fasten-off point of Row 33 of Main Section, work 38 sc evenly around neck edge to top of dc at end of Row 32, working through both ruffle formed by Rows 28 and 29 and rows underneath, ch 61 (for 2nd tie), 1 sc into 2nd ch from hook, 1 sc into each of next 59 ch, 1 sc into each of next 38 sc, 1 sc into each of next 60 ch, turn.

Next row Ch 1 (does not count as st), 1 sc into each sc to end.

Fasten off. Weave in yarn ends.

Duffle Coat and Hat

Using only double crochet stitches, you can make this duffle coat with its matching hat to delight any little girl. Choose a colorful hand-dyed wool tape yarn to create a bright multicolored effect.

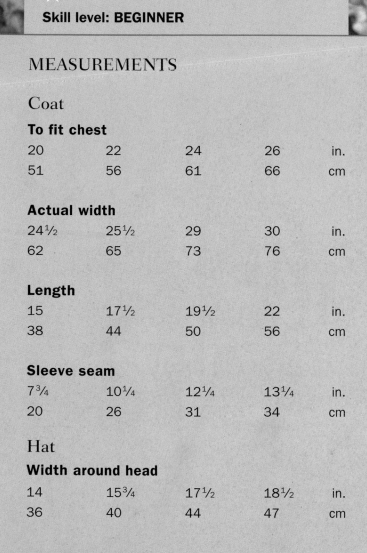

★ Skill level: BEGINNER

MEASUREMENTS

Coat

To fit chest

20	22	24	26	in.
51	56	61	66	cm

Actual width

24½	25½	29	30	in.
62	65	73	76	cm

Length

15	17½	19½	22	in.
38	44	50	56	cm

Sleeve seam

7¾	10¼	12¼	13¼	in.
20	26	31	34	cm

Hat
Width around head

14	15¾	17½	18½	in.
36	40	44	47	cm

MATERIALS

- 4 (5:5:6) × 100 g (3½ oz.) hanks of Colinette Tagliatelle in Jamboree 134 (Coat)

- 1 × 100 g (3½ oz.) hank of Colinette Tagliatelle in Jamboree 134 (Hat)

- J/10 (6.00 mm) crochet hook

- 3 toggle buttons, approximately 1 in. (2.5 cm) long

GAUGE

11 stitches and 7 rows to 4 in. (10 cm) measured over pattern, using J/10 (6.00 mm) hook. Change hook size, if necessary, to obtain this gauge.

ABBREVIATIONS

dc2tog—*yoh and insert hook as indicated, yoh and draw loop through, rep from * once more, yoh and draw through all 3 loops on hook.
See also page 11.

NOTE
Figures in parentheses refer to the larger sizes; where only one set of figures is given, this refers to all sizes.

COAT

BACK

Ch 36 (38:42:44).

Foundation row (RS) 1 dc into 4th ch from hook, 1 dc into each ch to end, turn. 34 (36:40:42) sts.

Cont in patt as follows:

Row 1 Ch 3 (counts as first dc), skip dc at base of 3 ch, *1 dc between dc just skipped and next dc, skip 1 dc, rep from * to end, working last dc between first dc and 3 ch at beg of previous row, turn.

This row forms patt.

Cont in patt for another 15 (18:21:24) rows, ending with a RS (WS:RS:WS) row.

Shape armholes

Next row Ss across and into 4th st, 1 ss between last dc worked into and next dc, ch 3 (counts as first dc), skip 1 dc, *1 dc between dc just skipped and next dc, skip 1 dc, rep from * until 5 sts rem at end of row, turn, leaving rem sts unworked. 26 (28:32:34) sts.

Cont in patt for another 8 (9:10:11) rows, ending with a WS row.

Fasten off, placing markers to either side of center 14 (14:16:16) sts to denote back neck.

LEFT FRONT

Ch 21 (22:24:25).

Work foundation row as given for Back. 19 (20:22:23) sts.

Cont in patt as given for Back for 16 (19:22:25) rows, ending with a RS (WS:RS:WS) row.

Shape armhole

Working shaping in same way as for Back, dec 4 sts at end (beg:end:beg) of next row. 15 (16:18:19) sts.

Cont in patt for another 8 (9:10:11) rows, ending with a WS row.

Fasten off, placing marker 6 (7:8:9) sts in from armhole edge to denote neck edge.

RIGHT FRONT

Work to match Left Front, reversing all shaping.

Do not fasten off at end of Right Front; set this ball of yarn to one side, as it will be used for Hood.

SLEEVES

Ch 18 (20:22:24).

Work foundation row as for Back. 16 (18:20:22) sts.

Cont in patt as for Back as follows:

Work 1 row.

Next row Ch 3 (counts as first dc), 1 dc into dc at base of 3 ch—1 st increased, 1 dc between dc just worked into and next dc, skip 1 dc, *1 dc between dc just skipped and next dc, skip 1 dc, rep from * to end, working last dc between first dc and 3 ch at beg of previous row, 1 dc into same place as last dc—1 st increased, turn.

Working all incs. as set by last row, cont as follows:

1st size

Inc 1 st at each end of next 2 rows, then on foll 3 alt rows. 28 sts.

2nd and 3rd sizes

Inc 1 st at each end of 2nd and every foll alt row until there are 26 sts, then on every foll 3rd row until there are (30:34) sts.

4th size

Inc 1 st at each end of 3rd and every foll 3rd row until there are 36 sts.

All sizes

Work another 5 rows straight, ending with a WS row.

Fasten off.

Place markers along row-end edges 1¼ in. (3.5 cm) down from top of last row to denote top of sleeve seam.

HOOD

Join shoulder seams.

With RS facing, using ball of yarn set to one side with Right Front, work around neck edge as follows:

Next row (RS) Work across sts of Right Front as follows: ch 3 (counts as first dc), skip dc at base of 3 ch, (1 dc between dc just skipped and next dc, skip 1 dc) 8 (8:9:9) times, 2 dc between dc just skipped and next dc, skip 1 dc, work across sts of back neck as follows: 2 dc between first 2 dc, (1 dc between next 2 dc, 2 dc between next 2 dc) 3 times, (1 dc between each of next 2 dc) 0 (0:1:1) times, (2 dc between next 2 dc, 1 dc between next dc) 3 times, 2 dc between last 2 dc, work across sts of Left Front as follows: 2 dc between first 2 dc, (1 dc between next 2 dc) 9 (9:10:10) times, turn. 44 (44:48:48) sts.

Work in patt as for Back for 7 (8:9:10) rows.

Next row Patt 20 (20:22:22) sts, (dc2tog over next 2 sts) twice, patt 20 (20:22:22) sts, turn.

Next row Patt 19 (19:21:21) sts, (dc2tog over next 2 sts) twice, patt 19 (19:21:21) sts, turn.

Next row Patt 18 (18:20:20) sts, (dc2tog over next 2 sts) twice, patt 18 (18:20:20) sts, turn.

Next row Patt 17 (17:19:19) sts, (dc2tog over next 2 sts) twice, patt 17 (17:19:19) sts, turn.

Next row Patt 16 (16:18:18) sts, (dc2tog over next 2 sts) twice, patt 16 (16:18:18) sts, turn. 34 (34:38:38) sts.

Fold Hood in half so that RS are together and close top seam of Hood by working a row of sc, working each st through both layers.

Fasten off. Weave in yarn ends.

FRONT OPENING, HOOD, AND HEM EDGING

Join side seams.

With RS facing, rejoin yarn at base of one side seam, ch 1 (does NOT count as st), work 1 round of sc evenly around entire hem, front opening, and hood edges, working 3 sc into hem corners and ending with ss to first sc, do NOT turn.

Now work 1 round of crab st (see page 21) around entire outer edge, ending with ss to first sc.

Fasten off. Weave in yarn ends.

CUFF EDGINGS

Join sleeve seams below markers. Matching top of sleeve seam to top of side seam and center of top of last row of sleeve to shoulder seam, sew sleeves into armholes.

Work edging around lower edges of sleeves in same way as for front, hood, and hem edging, rejoining yarn at base of sleeve seam.

FINISHING

Sew on toggle buttons 1¼ in. (3 cm) in from finished edge, placing top button 3 in. (8 cm) below first row of hood, lowest button 5½ (6¼:7:8) in. (14 [16:18:20] cm) up from lower edge, and third button midway between. Use "holes" of pattern as buttonholes.

HAT

Ch 8 and work a ss into 4th ch from hook to form a ring (leave rem 4 ch free for loop).

Round 1 (RS) Ch 3 (counts as first dc), 7 dc into ring, ss into top of 3 ch at beg of round, turn. 8 sts.

Round 2 Ss between first 2 dc, ch 3 (counts as first dc), 1 dc into same place as ss, (1 dc between next 2 dc, 2 dc between next 2 dc) 3 times, 1 dc between next 2 dc, ss to top of 3 ch at beg of round, turn. 12 sts.

Round 3 Ss between first 2 dc, ch 3 (counts as first dc), 1 dc into same place as ss, (2 dc between next 2 dc) 11 times, ss to top of 3 ch at beg of round, turn. 24 sts.

Round 4 Ss between first 2 dc, ch 3 (counts as first dc), 1 dc into same place as ss, *(1 dc between next 2 dc) twice**, 2 dc between next 2 dc, rep from * to end, ending last rep at **, ss to top of 3 ch at beg of round, turn. 32 sts.

Round 5 Ss between first 2 dc, ch 3 (counts as first dc), 1 dc into same place as ss, *(1 dc between next 2 dc) 3 times**, 2 dc between next 2 dc, rep from * to end, ending last rep at **, ss to top of 3 ch at beg of round, turn. 40 sts.

2nd size only

Round 6 Ss between first 2 dc, ch 3 (counts as first dc), 1 dc into same place as ss, *(1 dc between next 2 dc) 9 times**, 2 dc between next 2 dc, rep from * to end, ending last rep at **, ss to top of 3 ch at beg of round, turn. 44 sts.

3rd and 4th sizes only

Round 6 Ss between first 2 dc, ch 3 (counts as first dc), 1 dc into same place as ss, *(1 dc between next 2 dc) 4 times**, 2 dc between next 2 dc, rep from * to end, ending last rep at **, ss to top of 3 ch at beg of round, turn. 48 sts.

4th size only

Round 7 Ss between first 2 dc, ch 3 (counts as first dc), 1 dc into same place as ss, *(1 dc between next 2 dc) 11 times**, 2 dc between next 2 dc, rep from * to end, ending last rep at **, ss to top of 3 ch at beg of round, turn. 52 sts.

All sizes

Next round Ss between first 2 dc, ch 3 (counts as first dc), (1 dc between next 2 tdc) to end, ss to top of 3 ch at beg of round, turn.

Rep last round 3 (3:4:4) times more.

Next round Ch 1 (does not count as st), 1 sc into each dc to end, ss to first sc, do not turn.

Now work 1 round of crab st (see page 21) around entire edge.

Fasten off.

Fold 4 ch at top of hat (base of foundation ring) in half, and sew in place. Weave in all yarn ends.

A hood keeps little ones cozy.

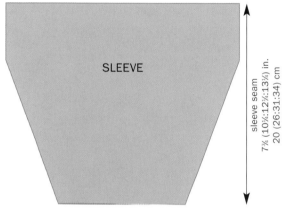

SLEEVE

sleeve seam
7¾ (10¼:12¼:13¼) in.
20 (26:31:34) cm

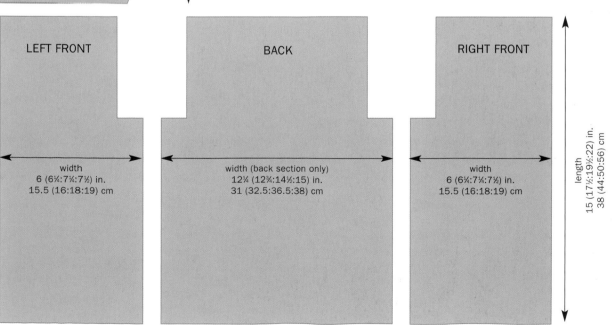

LEFT FRONT

width
6 (6¼:7¼:7½) in.
15.5 (16:18:19) cm

BACK

width (back section only)
12¼ (12¾:14½:15) in.
31 (32.5:36.5:38) cm

RIGHT FRONT

width
6 (6¼:7¼:7½) in.
15.5 (16:18:19) cm

length
15 (17½:19½:22) in.
38 (44:50:56) cm

Soft-Touch Baby Afghan

Created in the softest of brushed yarns, this cuddly blanket will soon become a favorite for baby! Worked in just single and double crochet, with simple bobble decoration, it's quick and easy to make.

Skill level: BEGINNER

MEASUREMENTS

27½ × 39½ in.
70 × 100 cm

MATERIALS

- 7 × 50 g (1¾ oz.) balls of Rowan Soft Baby in Meadow 007

- H/8 (5.00 mm) crochet hook

GAUGE

12½ stitches and 9½ rows to 4 in. (10 cm) measured over pattern on H/8 (5.00 mm) hook. Change hook size, if necessary, to obtain this gauge.

ABBREVIATIONS

sc2tog—[insert hook into next st, yoh and draw loop through] twice, yoh and draw through all 3 loops on hook.
dc4tog—*yoh and insert hook as indicated in patt instructions, (yoh and draw loop through), rep from * 3 times more, yoh and draw through all 5 loops on hook.
See also page 11.

Ch 79.
Foundation row (RS) 1 dc into 4th ch from hook, 1 dc into each ch to end, turn. 77 sts. Cont in patt as follows:
Row 1 Ch 1 (does NOT count as st), 1 sc into each of first 2 dc, *dc4tog into next dc, 1 sc into each of next 3 dc, rep from * to last 3 sts, dc4tog into next dc, 1 sc into next dc, 1 sc into top of 3 ch at beg of previous row, turn.
Row 2 Ch 3 (counts as first dc), skip sc at base of 3 ch, 1 dc into each st to end, turn.
Row 3 Ch 1 (does NOT count as st), 1 sc into each of first 4 dc, dc4tog into next dc, 1 sc into each of next 3 dc, rep from * to end, working last sc into top of 3 ch at beg of previous row, turn.
Row 4 As Row 2.
These 4 rows form patt. Work in patt for another 82 rows, ending with a patt row 2 and with RS facing for next row. (This section should measure 24½ × 36½ in. [62 × 92 cm].) Do not fasten off.

BORDER

With RS facing, work around entire outer edge of main section as follows: ch 1 (does not count as st), 2 sc into first (corner) dc, 1 sc into each of next 24 dc, sc2tog over next 2 dc, 1 sc into each of next 23 dc, sc2tog over next 2 dc, 1 sc into each of next 24 dc, 3 sc into top of 3 ch at beg of previous row, work 111 sc evenly down row end edge, 3 sc into ch at end of foundation row, 1 sc into each of next 24 ch, sc2tog over next 2 ch, 1 sc into each of next 23 ch, sc2tog over next 2 ch, 1 sc into each of next 24 ch, 3 sc into ch at beg of foundation row, work 111 sc evenly up other row-end edge, 1 sc into same place as sc at beg of round, ss to first sc, turn. 380 sts.

Next round Ch 1 (does not count as st), 1 sc into each of first 113 sc, 3 sc into next corner sc, 1 sc into each of next 75 sc, 3 sc into next corner sc, 1 sc into each of next 113 sc, 3 sc into next corner sc, 1 sc into each of next 75 sc, 3 sc into last corner sc, ss to first sc, do not turn. 388 sts.

Next round (WS) Ch 1 (does not count as st), 1 sc into first sc, *dc4tog into next sc, 1 sc into each of next 3 sc, rep from * to end, working (1 sc, dc4tog, and 1 sc) into each corner sc and ending last rep with 1 sc in last sc—first of these 2 sc is a corner sc, ss to first sc, do not turn.

Next round Ch 1 (does NOT count as st), 1 sc into each st to end, working 3 sc into each corner dc4tog and ending with ss to first sc, turn.

Next round Ch 1 (does NOT count as st), 1 sc into each st to end, working 3 sc into each corner sc and ending with ss to first sc, turn.

Rep last round once more. Fasten off. Weave in yarn ends.

FINISHING

Press carefully, following instructions on yarn label.

Fisherman's Sweater

Combine the simplest of shapes with the simplest of textured stitches to create this everyday sweater any child will enjoy wearing. Worked in a soft pure cotton yarn that is machine washable, it will stay looking good for a long time.

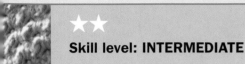

Skill level: INTERMEDIATE

MEASUREMENTS

To fit chest

20	22	24	26	in.
51	56	61	66	cm

Actual width

23	25	27	29	in.
58	63	68	74	cm

Length

12¼	13¾	15¾	17½	in.
31	35	40	44	cm

Sleeve seam

7½	9	10½	12¼	in.
19	23	27	31	cm

MATERIALS

- 8 (8:9:10) × 50 g (1¾ oz.) balls of Twilleys Freedom Cotton in pale gray 5

- G/6 (4.25 mm) crochet hook

GAUGE

15½ sts and 16 rows to 4 in. (10 cm) measured over pattern using G/6 (4.25 mm) hook. Change hook size, if necessary, to obtain this gauge.

ABBREVIATIONS

sc2tog—[insert hook as indicated, yarn over hook and draw loop through] twice, yarn over hook and draw through all 3 loops on hook.
See also page 11.

NOTE
Figures in parentheses refer to the larger sizes; where only one set of figures is given, this refers to all sizes.

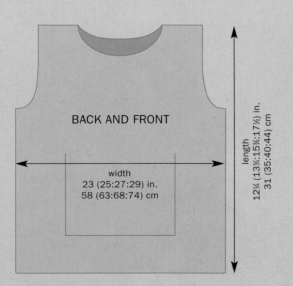

BACK AND FRONT

width
23 (25:27:29) in.
58 (63:68:74) cm

length
12¼ (13¾:15¾:17½) in.
31 (35:40:44) cm

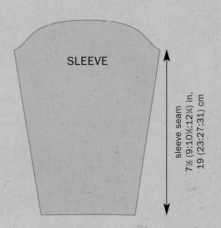

SLEEVE

sleeve seam
7½ (9:10½:12¼) in.
19 (23:27:31) cm

SWEATER

BACK

Ch 46 (50:54:58).

Foundation row (RS) 1 sc into 2nd ch from hook, 1 sc into each ch to end, turn. 45 (49:53:57) sts.

Cont in patt as follows:

Row 1 Ch 1 (does NOT count as st), 1 sc into first sc, *1 tr into next sc, 1 sc into next sc, rep from * to end, turn.

Row 2 Ch 1 (does NOT count as st), 1 sc into each sc and tr to end, turn.

Row 3 Ch 1 (does not count as st), 1 sc into each of first 2 sc, * 1 tr into next sc, 1 sc into next sc, rep from * to last sc, 1 sc into last sc, turn.

Row 4 As Row 2.

These 4 rows form patt.

**Cont in patt until Back measures $7\frac{1}{2}$ ($8\frac{1}{2}$:$10\frac{1}{4}$:$11\frac{1}{2}$) in. (19 [22:26:29] cm), ending with a WS row.

Shape armholes

Place markers at both ends of last row to denote base of armholes.

Next row Ch 1 (does not count as st), sc2tog over first 2 sts—1 st decreased, patt to last 2 sts, sc2tog over last 2 sts—1 st decreased, turn.

Rep last row 5 times more. 33 (37:41:45) sts. Cont in patt until armholes measure 4 ($4\frac{1}{4}$:$4\frac{3}{4}$:5) in., (10 [11:12:13] cm), ending with a WS row.

Shape back neck

Next row (RS) Ch 1 (does NOT count as st), 1 sc into each of first 9 (10:11:12) sts, turn, leaving rem sts unworked.

Work on these sts only for first side of neck.

Dec 1 st at neck edge on next 2 rows, ending with a RS row. 7 (8:9:10) sts.

Fasten off.

Return to last complete row worked, skip center 15 (17:19:21) sts, rejoin yarn to next st with RS facing, ch 1 (does NOT count as st), 1 sc into st where yarn was rejoined, 1 sc into each st to end, turn. 9 (10:11:12) sts. Complete second side to match first.

FRONT

Work as for Back until Front measures 2(2:$2\frac{1}{2}$:$2\frac{1}{2}$) in. (5[5:6:6] cm), ending with a WS row.

Break yarn.

Place pouch pocket

Next row (RS) Skip first 11 (12:13:14) sts, rejoin yarn to front loop only of next st, ch 1 (does NOT count as st), working into front loops only: 1 sc into st where yarn was rejoined, 1 sc into each of next 22 (24:26:28) sts, turn.

Work another 15 (17:19:21) rows on these 23 (25:27:29) sts only for pocket front, ending with a WS row.

Break yarn.

Return to last complete row worked and rejoin yarn to first st with RS facing, ch 1 (does NOT count as st), 1 sc into st where yarn was rejoined (this is first st), 1 sc into each of next 10 (11:12:13) sts, 1 sc into back loop only of next 23 (25:27:29) sts (these are sts behind pocket front), 1 sc into each st to end, turn. 45 (49:53:57) sts.

Work another 15 (17:19:21) rows, ending with a WS row.

Join pocket

Next row (RS) Ch 1 (does NOT count as st), 1 sc into each of first 11 (12:13:14) sts, 1 sc into first st of pocket front and next st of previous row, (1 sc into next st of pocket front and next st of previous row) 22 (24:26:28) times, 1 sc into each st to end, turn. 45 (49:53:57) sts.

Work as for Back from ** until 9 (9:11:11) rows fewer have been worked than on Back to fasten off row, ending with a WS row.

Shape front neck

Next row (RS) Ch 1 (does NOT count as st), 1 sc into each of first 12 (13:15:16) sts, turn, leaving rem sts unworked.

Work on these sts only for first side of neck.

Dec 1 st at neck edge on next 5 rows, then on foll 0 (0:1:1) alt row. 7 (8:9:10) sts.

Work 3 rows, ending with a RS row.

Fasten off. Weave in yarn ends.

Return to last complete row worked, skip center 9 (11:11:13) sts, rejoin yarn to next st with RS facing, ch 1 (does NOT count as st), 1 sc into st where yarn was rejoined, 1 sc into each st to end, turn. 12 (13:15:16) sts. Complete second side to match first.

SLEEVES

Ch 26 (28:30:32).
Work foundation row as for Back. 25 (27:29:31) sts.
Cont in patt as for Back as follows:

Work 3 rows.

Next row (RS) Ch 1 (does NOT count as st), 2 sc into first sc—1 st increased, 1 sc into each st to last st, 2 sc into last st—1 st increased, turn.

Working all increases as set by last row, inc 1 st at each end of every foll 4th (4th:5th:5th) row until there are 37 (41:43:47) sts, taking inc sts into patt.

Cont straight until Sleeve measures 7½ (9:10½:12¼) in. (19 [23:27:31] cm), ending with a RS row.

Shape top
Place markers at both ends of last row to denote base of armholes.

Dec 1 st at each end of next 6 rows, ending with a RS row. 25 (29:31:35) sts.

Fasten off. Weave in yarn ends.

NECK BORDER

Join shoulder seams.

With RS facing, attach yarn at left shoulder seam and work around neck edge as follows:

Round 1 (RS) Ch 1 (does NOT count as st), 9 (9:11:11) sc down left side of front neck, 1 sc into each of 9 (11:11:13) sts skipped at center front, 9 (9:11:11) sc up right side of front neck, 3 sc down right side of back neck, 1 sc into each of 15 (17:19:21) sts skipped at center back, 3 sc up left side of back neck, ss to first sc, turn. 48 (52:58:62) sts.

Round 2 Ch 1 (does NOT count as st), *1 sc into next sc, 1 tr into next sc, rep from * to end, ss to first sc, turn.

Round 3 Ch 1 (does not count as st), 1 sc into each st to end, ss to first sc, turn.

Round 4 Ch 1 (does not count as st), *1 tr into next sc, 1 sc into next sc, rep from * to end, ss to first sc, turn.

Round 5 Ch 1 (does not count as st), 1 sc into each st to end, ss to first sc, turn.

Rounds 6 and 7 As Rounds 2 and 3.

Fasten off. Weave in yarn ends.

FINISHING

Sew sleeves into armholes, matching markers and center of top of last row of sleeves to shoulder seams. Sew side and sleeve seams.

The lovely stitch pattern makes this a sweater even grown-ups will want to copy.

Sunday Best

This stylish flared coat with matching hat combines clever flower motifs and simple single crochet fabric. Worked in a pure cotton yarn, the stripy edging complements and completes the look.

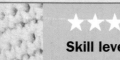

Skill level: ADVANCED

MEASUREMENTS

COAT
TO FIT CHEST

20	22	24	26	in.
51	56	61	66	cm

Actual width

23	25	27	29	in.
59	64	69	74	cm

Length

18	21	23	26	in.
46	54	58	66	cm

Sleeve seam

7½	9	10½	12¼	in.
19	23	27	31	cm

HAT
WIDTH AROUND HEAD

13¾	15¼	17¼	19	in.
35	39	44	48	cm

MATERIALS

- 5 (6: 7:7) × 100 g (3½ oz.) balls of Sirdar Pure Cotton DK in Cream 021 (A) (Coat)

- 1 × 100 g (3½ oz.) ball of Sirdar Pure Cotton DK in Cream 021 (Hat)

- 1 × 100 g (3½ oz.) ball of Sirdar Pure Cotton DK in Aqua Green 027 (B)

- 1 × 100 g (3½ oz.) ball of Sirdar Pure Cotton DK in Wisteria 032 (C)

- E/4 (3.50 mm) and G/6 (4.25 mm) crochet hooks

- 3 buttons, approximately ⅝ in. (15 mm) in diameter

GAUGE

16 sts and 18 rows to 4 in. (10 cm) measured over single crochet fabric using G/6 (4.25 mm) hook. Change hook size, if necessary, to obtain this gauge.

ABBREVIATIONS

sc2tog—[insert hook as indicated and draw loop through] twice, yarn over hook and draw through all 3 loops on hook.
See also page 11.

NOTE
Figures in parentheses refer to the larger sizes; where only one set of figures is given, this refers to all sizes.

The hat is made in rounds so in order to achieve the same look as the coat, you need to turn the work at the end of each round.

COAT

POCKET LININGS (MAKE 2)

Using larger hook and A, ch 12 (13:14:15).

Foundation row (RS) 1 sc into 2nd ch from hook, 1 sc into each ch to end, turn. 11 (12:13:14) sts.

Cont in sc as follows:

Row 1 Ch 1 (does NOT count as st), 1 sc into each sc to end, turn.

This row forms sc fabric.

Cont in sc fabric for another 12 (14:14:16) rows, ending with a WS row.

Fasten off. Weave in yarn ends.

BODY (worked in one piece to armholes)

Using larger hook and A, ch 122 (130:138:146).

Foundation row (RS) 1 sc into 2nd ch from hook, 1 sc into each ch to end, turn. 121 (129:137:145) sts.

Cont in sc as follows:

Row 1 Ch 1 (does NOT count as st), 1 sc into each sc to end, turn.

This row forms sc fabric.

Cont in sc fabric for another 4 rows, ending with a WS row.

Place flower motifs

Using a short length of B and C for each motif, cont as follows:

Row 1 (RS) Using A, ch 1 (does NOT count as st), 1 sc into each of first 8 sc, *remove hook from working loop and join in short length of B, using B (1 ss, ch 9, 1 ss, ch 10, 1 ss, ch 9, and 1 ss) all into next sc, fasten off B, pick up working loop, using A ch 1, skip sc worked into using B**, 1 sc into each of next 12 (13:14:15) sc, rep from * to end, ending last rep at **, 1 sc into each of last 8 sc, turn.

Row 2 Using A, ch 1 (does NOT count as st), 1 sc into each sc and ch sp to end, turn.

Row 3 Using A, ch 1 (does NOT count as st), 1 sc into each of first 5 sc, *1 sc into next sc enclosing 3rd loop of motif of Row 1 in st, 1 sc into each of next 5 sc, 1 sc into next sc enclosing first loop of motif of Row 1 in st**, 1 sc into each of next 6 (7:8:9) sc, rep from * to end, ending last rep at **, 1 sc into each of last 5 sc, turn.

Row 4 Using A, ch 1 (does NOT count as st), 1 sc into each sc to end, turn.

Row 5 Using A, ch 1 (does NOT count as st), 1 sc into each of first 8 sc, *remove hook from working loop and join in short length of C, enclosing 2nd loop of motif of Row 1 in sts, work (1 ss, ch 3, 4 dc, ch 3, and 1 ss) into next sc, fasten off C, pick up working loop, using A, ch 1, skip sc worked into using C**, 1 sc into each of next 12 (13:14:15) sc, rep from * to end, ending last rep at **, 1 sc into each of last 8 sc, turn.

Row 6 As Row 2.

Row 7 Using A, ch 1 (does NOT count as st), 1 sc into each of first 7 sc, *1 sc into next sc enclosing first 3 ch of motif of Row 5 in st, 1 sc into next sc, 1 sc into next sc enclosing last 3 ch of motif of Row 5 in st**, 1 sc into each of next 10 (11:12:13) sc, rep from * to end, ending last rep at **, 1 sc into each of last 7 sc, turn.

These 7 rows complete motif.

Cont in sc fabric using A as follows:

Work 3 rows, ending with a WS row.

Next row (RS) Ch 1 (does NOT count as st), 1 sc into each of first 11 (12:13:14) sc, [sc2tog over next 2 sc, 1 sc into each of next 14 (15:16:17) sc] 6 times, sc2tog over next 2 sc, 1 sc into each of last 12 (13:14:15) sc, turn. 114 (122:130:138) sts.

Work 11 (13:15:17) rows.

Next row (RS) Ch 1 (does NOT count as st), 1 sc into each of first 11 (12:13:14) sc, [sc2tog over next 2 sc, 1 sc into each of next 13 (14:15:16) sc] 6 times, sc2tog over next 2 sc, 1 sc into each of last 11 (12:13:14) sc, turn. 107 (115:123:131) sts.

Work 1 (5:7:11) rows.

Place pockets

Next row (RS) Ch 1 (does NOT count as st), 1 sc into each of first 8 (9:10:11) sc, 1 sc into each of the 11 (12:13:14) sc of first Pocket Lining, skip next 11 (12:13:14) sc of Body, 1 sc into each of next 69 (73:77:81) sc, 1 sc into each of the 11 (12:13:14) sc of 2nd Pocket Lining, skip next 11 (12:13:14) sc of Body, 1 sc into each of last 8 (9:10:11) sc, turn.

Work 9 (7:7:5) rows.

Next row (RS) Ch 1 (does NOT count as st), 1 sc into each of first 10 (11:12:13) sc, [sc2tog over next 2 sc, 1 sc into each of next 12 (13:14:15) sc] 6 times, sc2tog over next 2 sc, 1 sc into each of last 11 (12:13:14) sc, turn. 100 (108:116:124) sts.

Work 11 (13:15:17) rows.

Next row (RS) Ch 1 (does NOT count as st), 1 sc into each of first 10 (11:12:13) sc, [sc2tog over next 2 sc, 1 sc into each of next 11 (12:13:14) sc] 6 times, sc2tog over next 2 sc, 1 sc into each of last 10 (11:12:13) sc, turn. 93 (101:109:117) sts.

Cont in sc fabric until Body measures 12½ (15¼:16½:19¼) in. (32 [39:42:49] cm), ending with a WS row.

Divide for armholes

Next row (RS) Ch 1 (does NOT count as st), 1 sc into each of first 21 (23:25:27) sc, turn, leaving rem sts unworked.

Work on these 21 (23:25:27) sts only for Right Front.

Next row Ch 1 (does NOT count as st), sc2tog over first 2 sc, 1 sc into each sc to end, turn. 20 (22:24:26) sts.

Place flower motif

Using a short length of B and C for motif, cont as follows:

Row 1 (RS) Using A, ch 1 (does NOT count as st), 1 sc into each of first 8 (9:10:11) sc, remove hook from working loop and join in short length of B, using B (1 ss, ch 9, 1 ss, ch 10, 1 ss, ch 9, and 1 ss) all into next sc, fasten off B, pick up working loop, using A, ch 1, skip sc worked into using B, 1 sc into each of next 9 (10:11:12) sc, sc2tog over last 2 sts, turn.

Row 2 Using A, ch 1 (does NOT count as st), sc2tog over first 2 sts, 1 sc into each of next 8 (9:10:11) sc, 1 sc into next ch sp, 1 sc into each sc to end, turn. 18 (20:22:24) sts.

Row 3 Using A, ch 1 (does NOT count as st), 1 sc into each of first 5 (6:7:8) sc, 1 sc into next sc enclosing 3rd loop of motif of Row 1 in st, 1 sc into each of next 5 sc, 1 sc into next sc enclosing first loop of motif of Row 1 in st, 1 sc into each of next 4 (5:6:7) sc, sc2tog over last 2 sts, turn.

Row 4 Using A, ch 1 (does NOT count as st), sc2tog over first 2 sts, 1 sc into each sc to end, turn. 16 (18:20:22) sts.

Row 5 Using A, ch 1 (does NOT count as st), 1 sc into each of first 8 (9:10:11) sts, remove hook from working loop and join in short length of C, enclosing 2nd loop of motif of Row 1 in sts, work (1 ss, ch 3, 4 dc, ch 3, and 1 ss) into next sc, fasten off C, pick up working loop, using A, ch 1, skip sc worked into using C, 1 sc into each of last 7 (8:9:10) sc, turn.

Row 6 Using A, ch 1 (does NOT count as st), 1 sc into each of first 7 (8:9:10) sc, 1 sc into next ch sp, 1 sc into each sc to end, turn.

Row 7 Using A, ch 1 (does NOT count as st), 1 sc into each of first 7 (8:9:10) sc, 1 sc into next sc enclosing first 3 ch of motif of Row 5 in st, 1 sc into next sc, 1 sc into next sc enclosing last 3 ch of motif of Row 5 in st, 1 sc into each of last 6 (7:8:9) sc, turn.

These 7 rows complete motif.

**Cont in sc fabric using A as follows:

Cont straight until armhole measures 2¾ (3:3½:4) in. (7 [8:9:10] cm), ending at armhole edge.

Shape neck

Next row Ch 1 (does NOT count as st), 1 sc into each sc to last 4 (4:5:6) sts, turn, leaving rem sts unworked. 12 (14:15:16) sts.

Dec 1 st (by working sc2tog) at neck edge of next 4 rows, then on foll alt row. 7 (9:10:11) sts.

Cont straight until armhole measures 4¾ (5:5½:6) in. (12 [13:14:15] cm).

Fasten off.** Weave in yarn ends.

Shape back

Return to last complete row worked, skip next 4 sc, rejoin yarn to next sc and cont as follows:

Next row (RS) Ch 1 (does NOT count as st), 1 sc into sc where yarn was rejoined, 1 sc into each of next 42 (46:50:54) sc and turn, leaving rem sts unworked.

Cont on this set of 43 (47:51:55) sts only for Back. Dec 1 st (by working sc2tog) at each end of next 5 rows. 33 (37:41:45) sts.

Cont straight until Back matches Right Front to fasten off.

Fasten off, placing markers to either side of center 19 (19:21:23) sts to denote back neck.

Shape left front

Return to last complete row worked, skip next 4 sc, rejoin yarn to next sc and cont as follows:

Next row (RS) Ch 1 (does NOT count as st), 1 sc into sc where yarn was rejoined, 1 sc into each of sc to end, turn. 21 (23:25:27) sts.

Next row Ch 1 (does NOT count as st), 1 sc into each sc to last 2 sc, sc2tog over last 2 sc, turn. 20 (22:24:26) sts.

Place flower motif

Using a short length of B and C for motif, cont as follows:

Row 1 (RS) Using A, ch 1 (does NOT count as st), sc2tog over first 2 sts, 1 sc into each of next 9 (10:11:12) sc, remove hook from working loop and join in short length of B, using B, (1 ss, ch 9, 1 ss, ch 10, 1 ss, ch 9, and 1 ss) all into next sc, fasten off B, pick up working loop, using A, ch 1, skip sc worked into using B, 1 sc into each of last 8 (9:10:11) sc, turn.

Row 2 Using A, ch 1 (does NOT count as st), 1 sc into each of first 8 (9:10:11) sc, 1 sc into next ch sp, 1 sc into each sc to last 2 sts, sc2tog over last 2 sts, turn. 18 (20:22:24) sts.

Row 3 Using A, ch 1 (does NOT count as st), sc2tog over first 2 sts, 1 sc into each of next 4 (5:6:7) sc, 1 sc into next sc enclosing 3rd loop of motif of Row 1 in st, 1 sc into each of next 5 sc, 1 sc into next sc enclosing first loop of motif of Row 1 in st, 1 sc into each of last 5 (6:7:8) sc, turn.

Row 4 Using A, ch 1 (does NOT count as st), 1 sc into each sc to last 2 sts, sc2tog over last 2 sts, turn. 16 (18:20:22) sts.

Row 5 Using A, ch 1 (does NOT count as st), 1 sc into each of first 7 (8:9:10) sts, remove hook from working loop and join in short length of C, enclosing 2nd loop of motif of Row 1 in sts, work (1 ss, ch 3, 4 dc, ch 3, and 1 ss) into next sc, fasten off C, pick up working loop, using A, ch 1, skip sc worked into using C, 1 sc into each of last 8 (9:10:11) sc, turn.

Row 6 Using A, ch 1 (does NOT count as st), 1 sc into each of first 8 (9:10:11) sc, 1 sc into next ch sp, 1 sc into each sc to end, turn.

Row 7 Using A, ch 1 (does NOT count as st), 1 sc into each of first 6 (7:8:9) sc, 1 sc into next sc enclosing first 3 ch of motif of Row 5 in st, 1 sc into next sc, 1 sc into next sc enclosing last 3 ch of motif of Row 5 in st, 1 sc into each of last 7 (8 9:10) sc, turn.

These 7 rows complete motif.

Complete as given for Right Front from ** to **.

SLEEVES

Using larger hook and A, ch 28 (30:32:34).

Work foundation row as given for Body. 27 (29:31:33) sts.

Cont in sc fabric as follows:

Work 3 rows, ending with a WS row.

Next row (RS) Ch 1 (does NOT count as st), 2 sc into first sc—1 st increased, 1 sc into each sc to last st, 2 sc into last sc—1 st increased, turn. 29 (31:33:35) sts.

Working all increases as set by last row, cont as follows:

Work 1 row, ending with a WS row.

Place flower motif

Using a short length of B and C for motif, cont as follows:

Row 1 (RS) Using A, ch 1 (does NOT count as st), 1 sc into each of first 14 (15:16:17) sc, remove hook from working loop and join in short length of B, using B (1 ss, ch 9, 1 ss, ch 10, 1 ss, ch 9, and 1 ss) all into next sc, fasten off B, pick up working loop, using A, ch 1, skip sc worked into using B, 1 sc into each sc to end, turn.

Row 2 Using A, ch 1 (does NOT count as st), 1 sc into each of first 14 (15:16:17) sc, 1 sc into next ch sp, 1 sc into each sc to end, turn.

Row 3 Using A, ch 1 (does NOT count as st), 1 sc into each of first 11 (12:13:14) sc, 1 sc into next sc enclosing 3rd loop of motif of Row 1 in st, 1 sc into each of next 5 sc, 1 sc into next sc enclosing first loop of motif of Row 1 in st, 1 sc into each of sc to end, turn.

Row 4 Using A, ch 1 (does NOT count as st), 1 sc into each sc to end, turn.

Row 5 Using A, ch 1 (does NOT count as st), (2 sc into first sc) 1 (0:0:0) time, 1 sc into each of next 13 (15:16:17) sc, remove hook from working loop and join in short length of C, enclosing 2nd loop of motif of Row 1 in sts, work (1 ss, ch 3, 4 dc, ch 3, and 1 ss) into next sc, fasten off C, pick up working loop, using A, ch 1, skip sc worked into using C, 1 sc into each sc to last 1 (0:0:0) st, (2 sc into last sc) 1 (0:0:0) time, turn. 31 (31:33:35) sts.

Row 6 Using A, ch 1 (docs NOT count as st), 1 sc into each of first 15 (15:16:17) sc, 1 sc into next ch sp, 1 sc into each sc to end, turn.

Row 7 Using A, ch 1 (does NOT count as st), (2 sc into first sc) 0 (1:1:0) time, 1 sc into each of next 14 (13:14:16) sc, 1 sc into next sc enclosing first 3 ch of motif of Row 5 in st, 1 sc into next sc, 1 sc into next sc enclosing last 3 ch of motif of Row 5 in st, 1 sc into each sc to last 0 (1:1:0) st, (2 sc into last sc) 0 (1:1:0) time, turn. 31 (33:35:35) sts.

These 7 rows complete motif.

Cont in sc fabric using A as follows:

Inc 1 st at each end of 4th (10th:8th:2nd) and every foll 8th (10th:8th:10th) row until there are 35 (37:39:43) sts.

3rd size only

Inc 1 st at each end of foll 10th row. 41 sts.

All sizes

Cont straight until Sleeve measures $6\frac{1}{2}$ ($8\frac{1}{4}$:$9\frac{3}{4}$:$11\frac{1}{2}$) in. (17 [21:25:29] cm), ending with a WS row.

Shape top

Next row (RS) Ss across and into 3rd st, ch 1 (does NOT count as st), 1 sc into same place as last ss, 1 sc into each sc to last 2 sc, turn, leaving rem 2 sts unworked. 31 (33:35:39) sts.

Dec 1 st at each end of next 11 (12:13:14) rows. 9 (9:11:11) sts.

Fasten off. Weave in yarn ends.

HEM, FRONT OPENING, AND NECK EDGING

Join shoulder seams.

With RS facing, using smaller hook and A, rejoin yarn at lower edge at base of one side seam, ch 1 (does NOT count as st), work 1 round of sc evenly across hem edge, up right front opening edge, around neck edge, down left front opening edge, and across rem section of hem edge, working 3 sc into corners and ending with ss to first sc, turn.

Mark positions for 3 buttonholes along Right Front opening edge—first to come level with start of armhole

Pretty flower motifs embellish the coat and hat.

shaping, last to come level with neck shaping, and rem buttonhole evenly spaced between.

Next round (WS) Using B, ch 1 (does NOT count as st), 1 sc into each sc to end, making buttonholes at positions marked by replacing (1 sc into each of next 2 sc) with (ch 2, skip 2 sc), and skipping sc as required around neck edge to ensure that the edging lies flat, and working 3 sc into corners and ending with ss to first sc, turn.

Next round Using C, ch 1 (does NOT count as st), 1 sc into each sc to end, working 2 sc into each buttonhole ch sp, and skipping sc as required around neck edge to ensure that the edging lies flat, and working 3 sc into corners and ending with ss to first sc, turn.

Next round Using A, ch 1 (does NOT count as st), 1 sc into each sc to end, skipping sc as required around neck edge to ensure that the edging lies flat, and working 3 sc into corners, and ending with ss to first sc. Fasten off. Weave in yarn ends.

CUFF BORDERS (both alike)

With RS facing, using smaller hook and A, rejoin yarn to foundation ch edge of Sleeve, ch 1 (does NOT count as st), work 27 (29:31:33) sc evenly across foundation ch edge, turn.
******Next row (WS)** Using B, ch 1 (does NOT count as st), 1 sc into each sc to end, turn.
Next row Using C, ch 1 (does NOT count as st), 1 sc into each sc to end, turn.
Next row Using A, ch 1 (does NOT count as st), 1 sc into each sc to end, turn.

    Fasten off.

POCKET BORDERS (BOTH ALIKE)

With RS facing, using smaller hook and A, rejoin yarn to pocket opening edge, ch 1 (does NOT count as st), 1 sc into each of pocket opening 11 (12:13:14) sc, turn.

    Complete as for Cuff Borders from ****.

FINISHING

Join sleeve seams. Insert sleeves. Sew Pocket Linings in place on inside, then neatly sew down ends of Pocket Borders. Sew on buttons. Weave in all yarn ends.

HAT

Using larger hook and A, ch 56 (63:70:77) and join with a ss to form a ring.
Foundation round (RS) Ch 1 (does NOT count as st), 1 sc into each ch to end, ss to first sc, turn. 56 (63:70:77) sts.

    Cont in sc fabric as follows:
Round 1 Ch 1 (does NOT count as st), 1 sc into each sc to end, ss to first sc, turn.

    This round forms sc fabric.

    Work in sc fabric for another 2 rounds, ending with a WS round.

Place flower motif

Using a short length of B and C for motif, cont as follows:
Round 1 (RS) Using A, ch 1 (does NOT count as st), 1 sc into each of first 27 (31:34:38) sc, remove hook from working loop and join in short length of B, using B (1 ss, ch 9, 1 ss, ch 10, 1 ss, ch 9, and 1 ss) all into next sc, fasten off B, pick up working loop, using A, ch 1, skip sc worked into using B, 1 sc into each of next 28 (31:35:38) sc, ss to first sc, turn.
Round 2 Using A, ch 1 (does NOT count as st), 1 sc into each sc and ch sp to end, ss to first sc, turn.
Round 3 Using A, ch 1 (does NOT count as st), 1 sc into each of first 24 (28:31:35) sc, 1 sc into next sc enclosing 3rd loop of motif of Round 1 in st, 1 sc into each of next 5 sc, 1 sc into next sc enclosing first loop of motif of Round 1 in st, 1 sc into each of next 25 (28:32:35) sc, ss to first sc, turn.

    Work 1 round.

Round 5 Using A, ch 1 (does NOT count as st), 1 sc into each of first 27 (31:34:38) sc, remove hook from working loop and join in short length of C, enclosing 2nd loop of motif of Round 1 in sts, work (1 ss, ch 3, 4 dc, ch 3, and 1 ss) into next sc, fasten off C, pick up working loop, using A, ch 1, skip sc worked into using C, 1 sc into each of next 28 (31:35:38) sc, ss to first sc, turn.
Round 6 As Round 2.
Round 7 Using A, ch 1 (does NOT count as st), 1 sc into each of first 26 (30:33:37) sc, 1 sc into next sc enclosing first 3 ch of motif of Round 5 in st, 1 sc into next sc, 1 sc into next sc enclosing last 3 ch of motif of Round 5 in st, 1 sc into each of next 27 (30:34:37) sc, ss to first sc, turn.

    These 7 rounds complete motif.

    Cont in sc fabric using A as follows:

    Work 3 (3:5:5) rounds, ending with a WS round.

Shape crown

Round 1 (RS) Ch 1 (does NOT count as st), *sc2tog over next 2 sts, 1 sc into each of next 6 (7:8:9) sc, rep from * to end, ss to first sc2tog, turn. 49 (56:63:70) sts.

    Work 1 round.

Round 3 Ch 1 (does NOT count as st), *sc2tog over next 2 sts, 1 sc into each of next 5 (6:7:8) sc, rep from

* to end, ss to first sc2tog, turn. 42 (49:56:63) sts.

Work 1 round.

Round 5 Ch 1 (does NOT count as st), *sc2tog over next 2 sts, 1 sc into each of next 4 (5:6:7) sc, rep from * to end, ss to first sc2tog, turn. 35 (42:49:56) sts.

Work 1 round.

Round 7 Ch 1 (does NOT count as st), *sc2tog over next 2 sts, 1 sc into each of next 3 (4:5:6) sc, rep from * to end, ss to first sc2tog, turn. 28 (35:42:49) sts.

2nd, 3rd, and 4th sizes only

Work 1 round.

Round 9 Ch 1 (does NOT count as st), *sc2tog over next 2 sts, 1 sc into each of next (3:4:5) sc, rep from * to end, ss to first sc2tog, turn. (28:35:42) sts.

3rd and 4th sizes only

Work 1 round.

Round 11 Ch 1 (does NOT count as st), *sc2tog over next 2 sts, 1 sc into each of next (3:4) sc, rep from * to end, ss to first sc2tog, turn. (28:35) sts.

4th size only

Work 1 round.

Round 13 Ch 1 (does NOT count as st), *sc2tog over next 2 sts, 1 sc into each of next 3 sc, rep from * to end, ss to first sc2tog, turn. 28 sts.

All sizes

Next round (WS) Ch 1 (does NOT count as st), *sc2tog over next 2 sts, 1 sc into each of next 2 sc, rep from * to end, ss to first sc2tog, turn. 21 sts.

Next round Ch 1 (does NOT count as st), (sc2tog over next 2 sts, 1 sc into next sc) 7 times, ss to first sc2tog, turn. 14 sts.

Next round Ch 1 (does NOT count as st), (sc2tog over next 2 sts) 7 times, ss to first sc2tog, turn. 7 sts.

Next round Ch 1 (does NOT count as st), (sc2tog over next 2 sts) 3 times, 1 sc into next sc, ss to first sc2tog, turn. 4 sts.

Next round Ch 1 (does NOT count as st), (1 sc into next st) 4 times, do not turn.

Rep last round twice more.

Fasten off. Weave in yarn ends.

Lower Edging

With WS facing, using smaller hook and B, rejoin yarn to foundation ch edge, ch 1 (does NOT count as st), work 1 sc into each ch around foundation ch edge, ss to first sc, turn.

Next round Using C, ch 1 (does NOT count as st), 1 sc into each sc to end, ss to first sc, turn.

Next round Using A, ch 1 (does NOT count as st), 1 sc into each sc to end, ss to first sc, turn.

Fasten off. Weave in yarn ends.

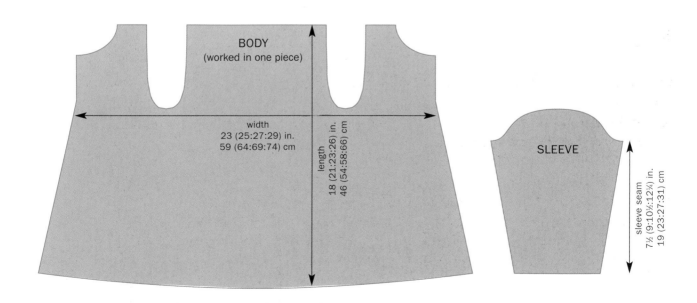

BODY
(worked in one piece)

width
23 (25:27:29) in.
59 (64:69:74) cm

length
18 (21:23:26) in.
46 (54:58:66) cm

SLEEVE

sleeve seam
7½ (9:10¾:12¼) in.
19 (23:27:31) cm

Hooded Sweater

This zipped, hooded sweater is worked in a textured cotton yarn. It features a simple stitch that is quick and easy to work. The embroidery on the pockets adds extra appeal.

Skill level: INTERMEDIATE

MEASUREMENTS

To fit ages

1–2	3–4	5–6	7–8	years

To fit chest

22	24	26	28	in.
56	61	66	71	cm

Actual width

25	27	29	31	in.
63	69	73	79	cm

Length from shoulder

13½	15½	17½	19½	in.
34	39	44	49	cm

MATERIALS

- 3 (4:5:6) × 50 g (1¾ oz.) hanks of Rowan Summer Tweed in Cape 511

- Small amounts of pink and green yarn for flower and leaves on pockets

- G/6 (4.25 mm) and H/8 (5.00 mm) crochet hooks

- Open-ended zipper approximately 11 (13:14:16) in. (28 [33:36:41] cm) long (see note)

GAUGE

12 sc and 7½ rows to 4 in. (10 cm) measured over double crochet pattern using H/8 (5.00 mm) crochet hook. Change hook size, if necessary, to obtain correct gauge.

ABBREVIATIONS

dc2tog—leaving the last loop of each st on hook, work 1 dc into each of the next 2 sts, yoh and draw through rem 3 loops on hook to dec 1 st.
See also page 11.

NOTE

Figures in parentheses refer to the larger sizes; where only one set of figures is given, this refers to all sizes. The details for the length of zipper required are guidelines only—it is always a good idea to purchase your zipper once the garment is made up so you can take an accurate measurement.

This quick-zip sweater is sure to be any little girl's favorite.

SWEATER

BACK

Using larger hook, ch 40 (43:46:49).

Foundation row 1 dc into 4th ch from hook, 1 dc in each ch to end, turn. 38 (41:44:47) sts.

Row 1 Ch 3 (counts as 1 dc), 1 dc in each dc, ending 1 dc in tch, turn.

Rep this row throughout.

Cont in patt until work measures 13 (15:17:19) in. (33 [38:43:48] cm) from beg.

Fasten off.

Mark the center 22 (23:24:25) sts for back neck.

LEFT FRONT

Using larger hook, ch 21 (23:24:26).

Foundation row Work as given for Back. 19 (21:22:24) sts.

Row 1 As given for Back.

Cont in patt until work measures 5 (5:5:6) rows shorter than Back to shoulder.

Shape neck

Row 1 Ss across and into the 9th (10th:10th:10th) st, ch 3 (counts as 1 dc), 1 dc in each st, ending 1 dc in tch, turn. 11 (12:13:15) sts.

Row 2 Ch 3 (counts as 1 dc), 1 dc in each st to last 3 sts, dc2tog, 1 dc in tch, turn.

Row 3 Ch 3 (counts as 1 dc), dc2tog, 1 dc in each st, ending 1 dc in tch, turn.

Row 4 As Row 2. 8 (9:10:12) sts.

4th size only

Row 5 As Row 3. 11 sts.

All sizes

Work 1 row. Fasten off. Weave in yarn ends.

RIGHT FRONT

Work as given for Left Front—patt is reversible.

POCKETS (make 2)

Using larger hook, ch 12 (14:16:18).

Foundation row Work as given for Back. 10 (12:14:16) sts.

Row 1 As given for Back.

Cont in patt until pocket measures 3 (3:3:3½) in. (8 [8:8:9] cm) from beg.

Change to smaller hook.

Next row Ch 1 (counts as 1 sc), 1 sc in each st, ending 1 sc in tch, turn.

Work 1 more row in sc. Fasten off. Weave in yarn ends.

HOOD

Join shoulders.

Using larger hook, ch 10 (11:11:11).

Foundation row As given for Back. 8 (9:9:9) sts.

Row 1 Ch 10 (11:11:12), 1 dc in 4th ch from hook, 1 dc in each ch and st, ending 1 dc in tch, turn. 16 (18:18:19) sts.

Row 2 Ch 3 (counts as 1 dc), 1 dc in each dc, ending 1 dc in tch, turn.

Row 3 Ch 10 (10:12:13), 1 dc into 4th ch from hook, 1 dc in each ch and st, ending 1 dc in tch, turn. 24 (26:28:30) sts.

Row 4 As Row 2.

Rep last row until work measures 15¾ (16½:17¼:18) in. (40 [42:44:46] cm) from last inc row, ending at shaped edge.

Next row Ss across and into the 9th (9th:11th:12th) st, ch 3 (counts as 1 dc), 1 dc in each st, ending 1 dc in tch, turn. 16 (18:18:19) sts.

Next row As Row 2.

Next row Ss across and into the 9th (10th:10th:11th) st, ch 3 (counts as 1 dc), 1 dc in each st, ending 1 dc in tch. 8 (9:9:9) sts. Fasten off.

Join shorter straight edge for back seam, then, with seam to center of back neck, sew to neck edge. Weave in yarn ends.

FINISHING

Mark a position 5½ (6:6¼:6½) in. (14 [15:16:17] cm) down from each side of shoulder seams for armhole positions. Sew side seams to markers. Weave in yarn ends.

Edges

With RS facing and using smaller hook, rejoin yarn at right side seam.

Next round Ch 1 (counts as 1 sc) work in sc evenly around edges, working 3 sc into each corner on lower fronts, sl st to 1 ch at beg, turn, and work 1 round in sc. Fasten off. Weave in yarn ends.

Armbands (both alike)

Using smaller hook, rejoin yarn at side seam.

Next round Ch 1 (counts as 1 sc), work in sc evenly around armhole edge, ss to 1 ch at beg, turn, and work 1 more round in sc. Fasten off.

Pockets and zipper

Position pockets on the center of each front, approximately 1 in. (3 cm) up from lower edge, and sew neatly in place. Sew zipper neatly in place to top of neck (see page 25). Weave in all yarn ends.

Flowers (make 4)

Using smaller hook and pink yarn, ch 6, ss to first ch to form a ring.

Next round (Ch 3, work 3 dc into ring, ch 3, ss to ring) 4 times. Fasten off, leaving a long end for sewing.

Leaves and stalks

Using smaller hook and green yarn, ch 12.

1st LEAF AND STALK 1 sc into 2nd ch from hook, 1 hdc into next ch, 1 dc into next ch, 1 hdc into next ch, 1 sc into next ch, ss to next ch.

Ch 6.

2nd LEAF AND STALK 1 sc into 2nd ch from hook, 1 hdc into next ch, 1 dc into next ch, 1 hdc into next ch, 1 sc into next ch, ss into same ch as ss on first leaf, ch 4. Fasten off.

Attach flowers and leaves to each pocket, so that the stalks lead to the flowers with leaves to either side.

Weave in yarn ends.

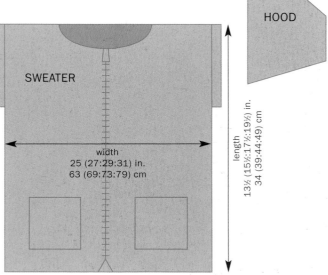

HOOD

SWEATER

width
25 (27:29:31) in.
63 (69:73:79) cm

length
13½ (15¼:17½:19½) in.
34 (39:44:49) cm

Itty-bitty Cardigan

Lacy stitches combine with simple double crochet stitches to create this pretty little cardigan. The yarn is easy care as well—simply wash and tumble dry as often as necessary.

★★

Skill level: INTERMEDIATE

MEASUREMENTS

To fit chest

20	22	24	26	in.
51	56	61	66	cm

Actual width

22	24	26	28	in.
56	61	66	71	cm

Length

11	12½	14½	16½	in.
28	32	37	42	cm

Sleeve seam

7¾	9	11	12¼	in.
20	23	28	31	cm

MATERIALS

• 3 (3:4:4) × 50 g (1¾ oz.) balls of Sirdar Snuggly 4 ply in Cream 303

• C/2 (2.50 mm) crochet hook

• 7 buttons, approximately ¼ in. (5 mm) in diameter

• sewing thread and needle

GAUGE

23 stitches and 12½ rows to 4 in. (10 cm) measured over double crochet fabric, using C/2 (2.50 mm) hook. Change hook size, if necessary, to obtain this gauge.

ABBREVIATIONS

dc2tog—[yoh, insert hook as indicated, yoh and draw loop through, yoh and draw through 2 loops] twice, yoh and draw through all 3 loops on hook.

picot—ch 3, 1 ss into dc just worked.

See also page 11.

NOTE

Figures in parentheses refer to the larger sizes; where only one set of figures is given, this refers to all sizes.

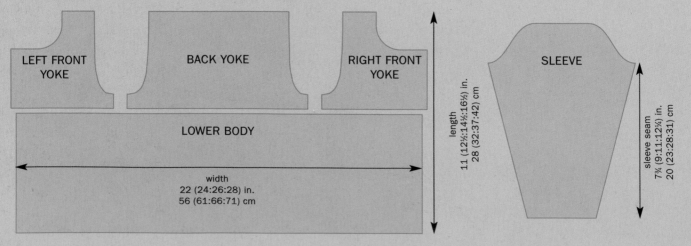

LEFT FRONT YOKE

BACK YOKE

RIGHT FRONT YOKE

SLEEVE

LOWER BODY

width
22 (24:26:28) in.
56 (61:66:71) cm

length
11 (12½:14½:16½) in.
28 (32:37:42) cm

sleeve seam
7¾ (9:11:12¼) in.
20 (23:28:31) cm

CARDIGAN

BACK YOKE

Ch 66 (72:78:84).

Foundation row (RS) 1 dc into 4th ch from hook, 1 dc into each ch to end, turn. 64 (70:76:82) sts.

Cont in dc fabric as follows:

Row 1 Ch 3 (counts as first dc), skip dc at base of 3 ch, 1 dc into each dc to end, working last dc into top of 3 ch at beg of previous row, turn.

Shape armholes

Next row (RS) Ss across and into 4th st, ch 3 (counts as first dc), skip dc at base of 3 ch, 1 dc into each dc to last 3 sts, turn, leaving rem 3 sts unworked. 58 (64:70:76) sts.

Next row Ch 3 (counts as first dc), skip dc at base of 3 ch, dc2tog over next 2 sts—1 st decreased, 1 dc into each dc to last 3 sts, dc2tog over next 2 sts—1 st decreased, 1 dc into top of 3 ch at beg of previous row, turn. ●

Rep last row 4 (5:5:6) times more. 48 (52:58:62) sts. Work another 8 (9:11:12) rows straight, ending with a WS row.

Choose pretty buttons in a matching color.

Fasten off, placing markers to either side of center 28 (30:32:34) sts to denote back neck.

LEFT FRONT YOKE

Ch 33 (36:39:42).

Work foundation row as given for Back.

31 (34:37:40) sts. Cont in dc fabric as follows:

Work 1 row.

Shape armhole

Next row (RS) Ss across and into 4th st, ch 3 (counts as first dc), skip dc at base of 3 ch, 1 dc into each dc to end, working last dc into top of 3 ch at beg of previous row, turn. 28 (31:34:37) sts.

Working all decreases in same way as for Back, dec 1 st at armhole edge on next 5 (6:6:7) rows. 23 (25:28:30) sts.

Work another 2 (3:3:4) rows straight, ending with a WS row.

Shape neck

Next row (RS) Ch 3 (counts as first dc), skip dc at base of 3 ch, 1 dc into each dc to last 9 (10:9:10) sts and turn, leaving rem 9 (10:9:10) sts unworked. 14 (15:19:20) sts.

Dec 1 st at neck edge on next 4 (4:6:6) rows. 10 (11:13:14) sts.

Work 1 row, ending with a WS row. Fasten off.

RIGHT FRONT YOKE

Work to match Left Front Yoke, reversing all shaping.

SLEEVES

Ch 37 (39:41:43).

Work foundation row as given for Back.

35 (37:39:41) sts. Cont in dc fabric as follows:

Work 1 row.

Next row (RS) Ch 3 (counts as first dc), 1 dc into st at base of 3 ch—1 st increased, 1 dc into each dc to last st, 2 dc into top of 3 ch at beg of previous row—1 st increased, turn.

Working all increases as set by last row, inc 1 st at each end of 4th (2nd:2nd:2nd) and every foll 3rd (3rd:3rd:alt) row until there are 47 (53:59:49) sts.

4th size only

Inc 1 st at each end of every foll 3rd row until there are 65 sts.

All sizes

Work another 5 rows straight, ending with a WS row.

Shape top

Next row (RS) Ss across and into 4th st, ch 3 (counts as first dc), skip dc at base of 3 ch, 1 dc into each dc to last 3 sts and turn, leaving rem 3 sts unworked. 41 (47:53:59) sts.

Dec 1 st at each end of next 7 (9:11:13) rows. 27 (29:31:33) sts. Fasten off.

LOWER BODY

Join shoulder seams. Join side seams.

With RS facing, rejoin yarn at base of Left Front Yoke opening edge, ch 1 (does NOT count as st), work 127 (136:145:163) sc evenly across lower edge of Left Front Yoke, Back Yoke, and Right Front Yoke to Right Front opening edge (this is 1 sc for each foundation ch skipping 0 [2:5:0] ch evenly spaced and inc 1 [0:0:1] st evenly), turn. 127 (136:145:163) sts.

Row 1 (WS) Ch 1 (does NOT count as st), 1 sc into first sc, *ch 5, skip 2 sc, 1 sc into next sc, rep from * to end, turn. 42 (45:48:54) ch sps.

Row 2 Ch 5 (counts as 1 dc and 2 ch), 1 sc into first ch sp, *8 dc into next ch sp, 1 sc into next ch sp**, ch 5, 1 sc into next ch sp, rep from * to end, ending last rep at **, ch 2, 1 dc into sc at beg of previous row, turn. 14 (15:16:18) patt repeats.

Row 3 Ch 1 (does NOT count as st), 1 sc into dc at end of previous row, skip (2 ch and 1 sc), *1 dc into next dc, (1 picot, 1 dc into next dc) 7 times, skip 1 sc**, 1 sc into next ch sp, skip 1 sc, rep from * to end, ending last rep at **, 1 sc into 3rd of 5 ch at beg of previous row, turn.

Row 4 Ch 8 (counts as 1 dc and 5 ch), skip (1 sc, 1 dc, 1 picot, 1 dc, 1 picot, and 1 dc), *1 sc into next picot, ch 5, skip (1 dc, 1 picot, and 1 dc), 1 sc into next picot, ch 5, skip (1 dc, 1 picot, 1 dc, 1 picot, and 1 dc), 1 dc into next sc**, ch 5, skip (1 dc, 1 picot, 1 dc, 1 picot, and 1 dc), rep from * to end, ending last rep at **, turn.

Rep Rows 2–4 3(4:5:6) more times, then Rows 2 and 3 again. Fasten off.

COLLAR

Ch 74 (82:82:82).

Row 1 (WS) 1 sc into 2nd ch from hook, *ch 5, skip 2 ch, 1 sc into next ch, ch 5, skip 1 ch, 1 sc into next ch, ch 5, skip 2 ch, 1 sc into next ch, rep from * to end, turn. 27 (30:30:30) ch sps, 9 (10:10:10) patt repeats.

Work Rows 2–4 as given for Lower Body once, then rep Rows 2 and 3 again. Fasten off.

FRONT OPENING AND NECK EDGING

Lay Collar against RS of Yoke, matching foundation ch of Collar to neck edge and row-end edges of Collar to front opening edges, and baste in place with sewing thread. With RS facing and working through both main sections and Collar around neck edge, rejoin yarn at lower edge of right front opening edge, ch 1 (does not count as st), work 1 row of sc evenly up right front opening edge, around neck edge, and down entire left front opening edge, working 3 sc into neck corners, turn.

Mark positions for 7 buttonholes along right front opening edge—the first 1¼ in. (3 cm) up from lower edge of lower body, the last level with neck shaping, and rem 5 buttonholes evenly spaced between.

Next row (WS) Ch 1 (does not count as st), 1 sc into each sc to end, making buttonholes at positions marked by replacing (1 sc into each of next 2 sc) with (ch 2, skip 2 sc), skipping sc as required around neck edge to ensure that the edging lies flat, and working 3 sc into neck corner points, turn.

Next row Ch 1 (does NOT count as st), 1 sc into each sc to end, working 2 sc into each buttonhole ch sp, skipping sc as required around neck edge to ensure that the edging lies flat, and working 3 sc into neck corner points.

Fasten off. Weave in all yarn ends.

CUFF EDGINGS

With RS facing, rejoin yarn to foundation ch edge of Sleeve, ch 1 (does not count as st), work 35 (37:39:41) sc evenly across foundation ch edge, turn.

Next row (WS) Ch 1 (does not count as st), 1 sc into each sc to end. Fasten off. Weave in all yarn ends.

FINISHING

Join sleeve seams. Insert sleeves. Sew on buttons.

Ribbons 'n' Bows Sweater

Baby gets a high-fashion look in this sweet little sweater trimmed with ribbon bows. The simple stitches combine with a pretty picot edge to give it a playful yet sophisticated look for little ones.

★★

Skill level: INTERMEDIATE

MEASUREMENTS

To fit chest

20	22	24	26	in.
51	56	61	66	cm

Actual width

23	24½	27	29	in.
58	62	69	74	cm

Length from shoulder

12¼	14	16	17½	in.
31	35	40	44	cm

Sleeve seam

8¼	10	11½	13	in.
21	25	29	33	cm

MATERIALS

- 2 (3:3:4) × 100 g (3½ oz.) hanks of Colinette Lasso in Morocco 127

- G/6 (4.25 mm) crochet hook

- 3¼ (3½:3⅝:3¾) yd. (3 [3.2:3.3:3.4] m) of ⅜-in. (1-cm) wide ribbon

- Safety pin or large needle for threading

GAUGE

17 stitches and 12 rows to 4 in. (10 cm) measured over half-double crochet fabric, using G/6 (4.25 mm) crochet hook. Change hook size, if necessary, to obtain this gauge.

ABBREVIATIONS

hdc2tog—[yoh and insert hook as indicated, yoh and draw loop through] twice, yoh and draw through all 5 loops on hook.
See also page 11.

NOTE

Figures in parentheses refer to the larger sizes; where only one set of figures is given, this refers to all sizes.

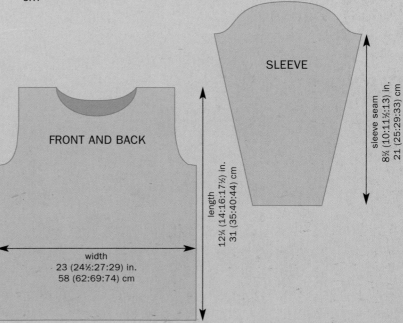

SLEEVE

sleeve seam
8¼ (10:11½:13) in.
21 (25:29:33) cm

FRONT AND BACK

length
12¼ (14:16:17½) in.
31 (35:40:44) cm

width
23 (24½:27:29) in.
58 (62:69:74) cm

SWEATER

BACK

Ch 50 [54:60:64].

Foundation row (RS) 1 hdc into 3rd ch from hook, 1 hdc into each ch to end, turn. 49 [53:59:63] sts.

Cont in hdc fabric as follows:

Row 1 Ch 2 (counts as first hdc), skip st at base of 2 ch, 1 hdc into each hdc to end, working last hdc into top of 2 ch at beg of previous row, turn.

This row forms hdc fabric.

Work another 4 rows.

Next row (RS) Ch 3 (counts as first hdc and 1 ch), skip st at base of 3 ch and next hdc, 1 hdc into next hdc, *ch 1, skip 1 hdc, 1 hdc into next hdc, rep from * to end, working last hdc into top of 2 ch at beg of previous row, turn.

Next row (WS) Ch 2 (counts as first hdc), skip st at base of 2 ch, 1 hdc into each hdc and ch sp to end, working last hdc into top of 2 ch at beg of previous row, turn.

Cont in hdc fabric (see Row 1 above) until Back measures 6½ (7¾:9½:10½) in. (17 [20:24:27] cm), ending with a WS row.

Shape armholes

Next row (RS) Ss across and into 4th st, ch 2 (counts as first hdc)—3 sts decreased, 1 hdc into each hdc to last 3 sts, turn, leaving last 3 sts unworked—3 sts decreased. 43 (47:53:57) sts.

Next row Ch 2 (does not count as st), skip st at base of 2 ch—1 st decreased, 1 hdc into each st to last 2 sts, hdc2tog over last 2 sts—1 st decreased, turn.

Rep last row 1 (1:2:2) more times.

Next row Ch 2 (does not count as st), skip st at base of 2 ch—1 st decreased, 1 hdc into next hdc, *ch 1, skip 1 hdc, 1 hdc into next hdc, rep from * to last 3 sts, ch 1, skip 1 hdc, hdc2tog over last 2 sts—1 st decreased, turn.

Next row Ch 2 (does not count as st), skip st at base of 2 ch—1 st decreased, 1 hdc into each hdc or ch sp to last 2 sts, hdc2tog over last 2 sts—1 st decreased, turn. 35 (39:43:47) sts.

Cont in hdc fabric until armholes measure 4 (4½:5:5¼) in. (10 [11.5:12.5:13.5] cm, ending with a WS row.

Shape back neck

Next row (RS) Ch 2 (counts as first hdc), 1 hdc into each of next 7 (9:9:10) sts, turn, leaving rem sts unworked.

Work on these 8 (9:10:11) sts only for first side of neck.

Dec 1 st at neck edge on next row, ending with a WS row. 7 (8:9:10) sts. Fasten off.

Return to last complete row worked, skip center 19 (21:23:25) sts, rejoin yarn to next st with RS facing, ch 2 (counts as first hdc), skip st where yarn was rejoined, 1 hdc into each st to end, turn. 8 (9:10:11) sts. Complete second side to match first side.

FRONT

Work as for Back until 6 (6:8:8) rows fewer have been worked than on Back to fasten off row, ending with a WS row.

Shape front neck

Next row (RS) Ch 2 (counts as first hdc), 1 hdc into each of next 10 (11:13:14) sts, turn, leaving rem sts unworked.

Work on these 11 (12:14:15) sts only for first side of neck.

Dec 1 st at neck edge on next 4 rows, then on foll 0 (0:1:1) alt row. 7 (8:9:10) sts.

Work 1 row, ending with a WS row.

Fasten off.

Return to last complete row worked, skip center 13 (15:15:17) sts, rejoin yarn to next st with RS facing, ch 2 (counts as first hdc), skip st where yarn was rejoined, 1 hdc into each st to end, turn. 11 (12:14:15) sts. Complete second side to match first.

SLEEVES

Ch 26 (28:30:32).

Work foundation row as for Back. 25 (27:29:31) sts.

Cont in hdc fabric as for Back as follows:

Work 1 row.

Row 3 (RS) Ch 2 (counts as first hdc), 1 hdc into st at base of 2 ch—1 st increased, 1 hdc into each st to last st, 2 hdc into top of 2 ch at beg of previous row—1 st increased, turn.

Working all increases as set by last row, inc 1 st at

each end of foll alt row. 29 (31:33:35) sts.

Work 1 row, ending with a WS row.

Row 7 (RS) Ch 2 (counts as first hdc), 1 hdc into st at base of 2 ch—1 st increased, *ch 1, skip 1 hdc, 1 hdc into next st, rep from * to last 2 sts, ch 1, skip 1 hdc, 2 hdc into top of 2 ch at beg of previous row—1 st increased, turn.

Row 8 Ch 2 (counts as first hdc), skip st at base of 2 ch, 1 hdc into each hdc and ch sp to end, working last hdc into top of 2 ch at beg of previous row, turn.

Inc 1 st at each end of next and foll 1 (1:1:0) alt row, then on every foll 4th row until there are 39 (43:47:51) sts.

Cont straight until Sleeve measures 7½ (9:10½:12¼) in. [19 (23:27:31) cm], ending with a WS row.

Shape top

Working all shaping in same way as for Back armholes, dec 3 sts at beg of next 2 rows. 33 (37:41:45) sts.

Dec 1 st at each end of next 8 (9:10:11) rows.

17 (19:21:23) sts. Fasten off. Weave in all yarn ends.

FINISHING

Join shoulder seams, side seams, and sleeve seams. Insert sleeves.

Edging

With RS facing, attach yarn at neckline of Left Front, ch 1 (does NOT count as st), work 1 round of sc evenly around entire neck edge, working a multiple of 3 sts and ending with ss to first sc, turn.

Next round Ch 1 (does NOT count as st), *1 sc into each of next 3 sc, ch 3, ss to sc just worked, rep from * to end, ss to first sc.

Fasten off. Weave in yarn ends.

Work Edging around lower edge of body and Sleeves in same way. Weave in yarn ends.

Using picture as a guide, thread ribbon through ch sps with a safety pin or needle and tie ends in bows.

The ribbon details make this sweater extra-special.

Ruffles Galore

Keep your toddler pretty in pink in this little bolero with ruffled edging. The main sections are worked in single crochet, and the edging combines both double crochet and chain stitches. Made in a soft cashmere-mix yarn, it's a touch of luxury for any little girl.

Skill level: BEGINNER

MEASUREMENTS

To fit chest

20	22	24	26	in.
51	56	61	66	cm

Actual width

21	24	26	28½	in.
54	61	66	72	cm

Length

9	10½	11½	13	in.
23	27	29	33	cm

Sleeve seam

7½	9	10¼	12¼	in.
19	23	26	31	cm

MATERIALS

- 5 (5:6:7) × 50 g (1¾ oz.) balls of Rowan RYC Cashsoft DK in Sweet 501
- G/6 (4.25 mm) crochet hook

GAUGE

18 stitches and 20 rows to 4 in. (10 cm) measured over single crochet fabric, using G/6 (4.25 mm) hook. Change hook size, if necessary, to obtain this gauge.

ABBREVIATIONS

sc2tog—[insert hook as indicated, yoh and draw loop through] twice, yoh and draw through all 3 loops on hook.
See also page 11.

NOTE

Figures in parentheses refer to the larger sizes; where only one set of figures is given, this refers to all sizes.

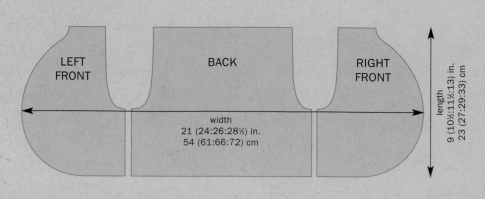

LEFT FRONT   BACK   RIGHT FRONT

width
21 (24:26:28½) in.
54 (61:66:72) cm

length
9 (10½:11½:13) in.
23 (27:29:33) cm

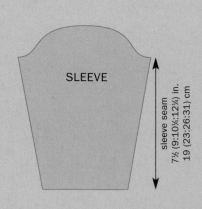

SLEEVE

sleeve seam
7½ (9:10¼:12¼) in.
19 (23:26:31) cm

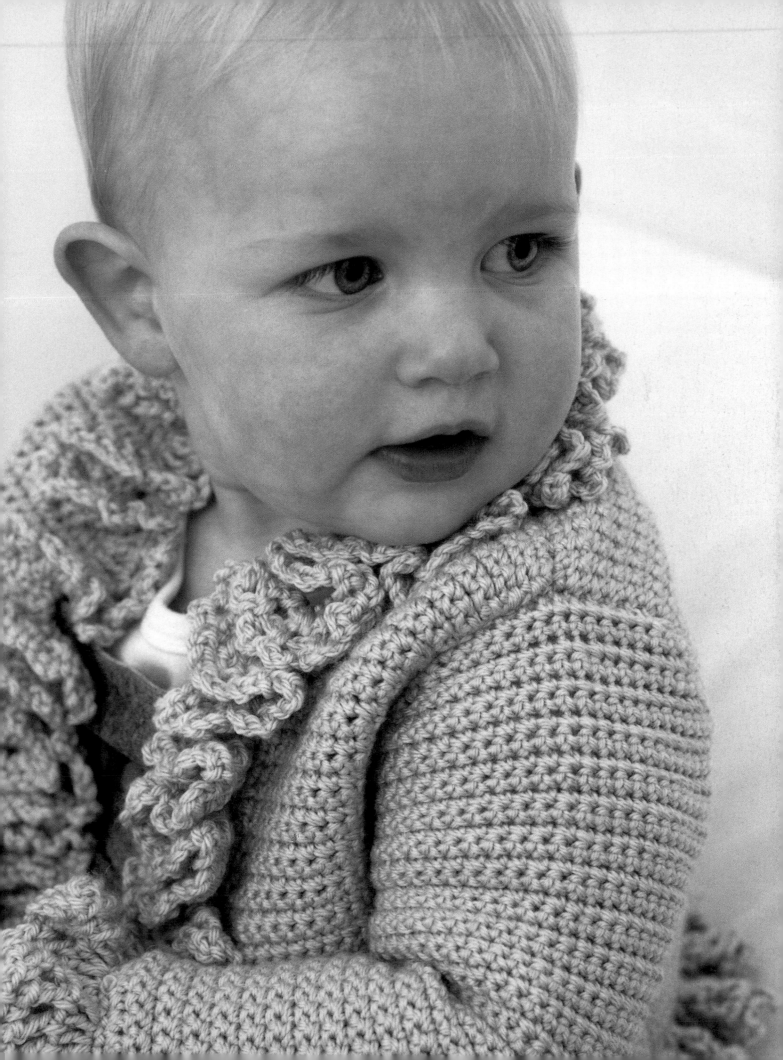

CARDIGAN

BACK

Ch 50 (56:60:66).

Foundation row (RS) 1 sc into 2nd ch from hook, 1 sc into each ch to end, turn. 49 (55:59:65) sts.

Cont in sc as follows:

Row 1 Ch 1 (does not count as st), 1 sc into each sc to end, turn.

This row forms sc fabric.

Cont in sc fabric for another 12 (18:20:26) rows.

Ruffles around the edges and cuffs offer a charming look.

Shape armholes

Next row (RS) Ss across and into 4th st, ch 1 (does NOT count as st), 1 sc into same sc as used for last ss, 1 sc into each sc to last 3 sc, turn, leaving rem 3 sts unworked. 43 (49:53:59) sts.

Next row Ch 1 (does NOT count as st), sc2tog over first 2 sts, 1 sc into each sc to last 2 sts, sc2tog over last 2 sts, turn.

Rep last row 2 (3:3:4) times more. 37 (41:45:49) sts.

Work another 20 (21:23:24) rows straight, ending with a WS row.

Fasten off, placing markers to either side of center 21 (21:23:25) sts to denote back neck.

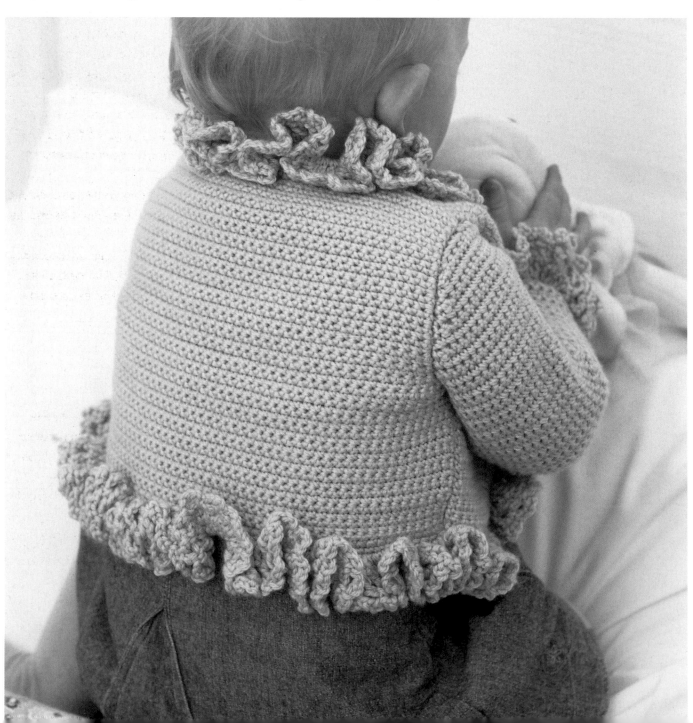

LEFT FRONT

Ch 14 (13:14:13).

Work foundation row as for Back. 13 (12:13:12) sts.

Next row (WS) Ch 1 (does not count as st), 2 sc into first sc—1 st increased, 1 sc into each sc to end, turn.

Next row Ch 1 (does not count as st), 1 sc into each sc to last sc, 2 sc into last sc—1 st increased, turn.

Working all increases as set by last 2 rows, inc 1 st at front opening edge on next 8 (10:10:12) rows, then on foll 1 (3:4:6) alt rows. 24 (27:29:32) sts.

Work 1 row, ending with a WS row.

Shape armhole

Next row (RS) Ss across and into 4th st, ch 1 (does not count as st), 1 sc into same sc as used for last ss, 1 sc into each sc to end, turn. 21 (24:26:29) sts.

Shape front slope

Working all decreases in same way as for Back armhole decreases, dec 1 st at armhole edge on next 3 (4:4:5) rows and at the same time dec 1 st at front slope edge on next and foll 1 (1:1:2) alt rows. 16 (18:20:21) sts.

Dec 1 st at front slope edge only on 2nd (next:next:2nd) and foll 5 (3:4:4) alt rows, then on every foll 3rd row until there are 8 (10:11:12) sts.

Work another 2 rows straight, ending with a WS row.
Fasten off.

RIGHT FRONT

Work to match Left Front, reversing all shaping.

SLEEVES

Ch 28 (30:32:34).

Work foundation row as for Back. 27 (29:31:33) sts. Cont in sc fabric as for Back for 3 rows.

Working all increases in same way as for front opening edge increases, inc 1 st at each end of next and every foll 5th row until there are 33 (35:37:37) sts, then on every foll 6th row until there are 37 (41:45:49) sts.

Work another 3 (5:5:8) rows straight, ending with a WS row.

Shape top

Next row (RS) Ss across and into 4th st, ch 1 (does not count as st), 1 sc into same sc as used for last ss, 1 sc into each sc to last 3 sc, turn, leaving rem 3 sts unworked. 31 (35:39:43) sts.

Dec 1 st at each end of next 9 (11:13:15) rows. 13 sts.

Fasten off. Weave in yarn ends.

FRONT AND HEM RUFFLE

Join shoulder seams. Join side seams.

With RS facing, rejoin yarn at base of one side seam, ch 1 (does not count as st), work 1 round of sc evenly across hem edge, up shaped right front opening edge, up right front slope, across back neck, down left front slope, around shaped left front opening edge, then across rem section of hem edge, ending with ss to first sc.

Next round Ch 1 (does NOT count as st), 1 sc into each sc to end, inc and dec sc as required to ensure that the edging lies flat and ending with ss to first sc.

*****Next round** Ch 4 (counts as 1 dc and 1 ch), 1 dc into st at base of 4 ch, *ch 1**, (1 dc, ch 1, and 1 dc) into next sc, rep from * to end, ending last rep at **, ss to 3rd of 4 ch at beg of round.

Next round Ss into first ch sp, ch 5 (counts as 1 dc and 2 ch), *1 dc into next ch sp, ch 2, rep from * to end, ss to 3rd of 5 ch at beg of round.

Next round Ss into first ch sp, ch 1 (does not count as st), 1 sc into same ch sp, *ch 4, 1 sc into next ch sp, rep from * to end, replacing sc at end of last rep with ss to first sc.

Fasten off. Weave in yarn ends.

CUFF RUFFLES

Join sleeve seams.

With RS facing, rejoin yarn at base of one sleeve seam, ch 1 (does not count as st), work 1 round of sc evenly around lower edge of Sleeve, ending with ss to first sc.

Next round Ch 1 (does not count as st), 1 sc into each sc to end, ending with ss to first sc.

Complete as given for Front and Hem Ruffle from ***.

FINISHING

Insert sleeves.

Weave in yarn ends.

All Zipped Up

Your little one will be snug and warm in this zippered cardigan with pockets. Two strands of soft yarn are worked together throughout the garment, so it is easy to make in a short amount of time.

★★

Skill level: INTERMEDIATE

MEASUREMENTS

To fit age

1–2	3–4	5–6	7–8	years

To fit chest

22	24	26	28	in.
56	61	66	71	cm

Actual width

25	27	28½	31	in.
63	69	73	79	cm

Length from shoulder

13¼	15¼	17¼	19	in.
34	39	44	48	cm

Sleeve seam (adjustable)

10	11¾	13½	15	in.
25	30	34	38	cm

MATERIALS

- 6 (7:8:9) × 50 g (1¾ oz.) balls of Rowan Calmer in Blush 477

- H/8 (5.00 mm) and J/10 (6.00 mm) crochet hooks

- Open-ended zipper, approximately 10 (12:14:16) in. [26:31:36:41] cm long (see notes)

- Matching sewing thread and sewing needle

GAUGE

12 sts and 10 rows to 4 in. (10 cm) measured over half-double crochet, using J/10 (6.00 mm) crochet hook. Change hook size, if necessary, to obtain this gauge.

ABBREVIATIONS

hdc2tog—[yoh, insert hook as indicated, yoh and draw loop through] twice, yoh and draw through all 5 loops on hook. *See also page 11.*

NOTES

Figures in parentheses refer to the larger sizes; where only one set of figures is given, this refers to all sizes.

The details for the length of zipper required are guidelines only—it is always a good idea to purchase your zipper once the garment is made up, so you can take an accurate measurement.

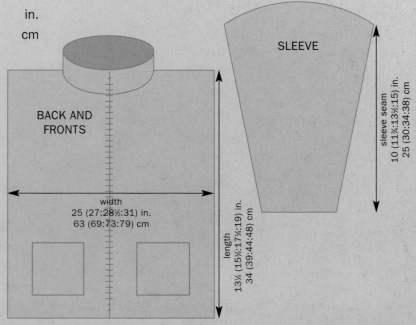

BACK AND FRONTS

SLEEVE

sleeve seam
10 (11¾:13½:15) in.
25 (30:34:38) cm

width
25 (27:28½:31) in.
63 (69:73:79) cm

length
13¼ (15¼:17¼:19) in.
34 (39:44:48) cm

JACKET

BACK

Using larger hook and 2 strands of yarn tog, ch 39 (42:45:48).

Foundation row 1 hdc into 3rd ch from hook, 1 hdc in each ch to end. 38 (41:44:47) sts.

Row 1 Ch 2 (counts as 1 hdc), 1 hdc in each st, ending 1 hdc in tch, turn.

Rep this row throughout.

Cont until work measures 13 (15:17:18½) in. (33 [38:43:47] cm) from beg. Fasten off.

Mark the center 22 (23:24:25) sts for back neck.

Check your measurements before inserting the zipper.

LEFT FRONT

Using larger hook and 2 strands of yarn tog, ch 20 (22:23:25).
Foundation row As given for Back. 19 (21:22:24) sts.
Row 1 As given for Back.
Cont until work measures 7 (7:7:9) rows shorter than Back to shoulder.

Shape neck

Next row Ss across and into the 7th (8th:8th:8th) st, ch 2 (counts as 1 hdc), 1 hdc into each st ending 1 hdc in tch, turn. 13 (14:15:17) sts.
Next row Ch 2 (counts as 1 hdc), 1 hdc in each st to last 3 sts, hdc2tog, 1 hdc in tch, turn.
Next row Ch 2 (counts as 1 hdc), hdc2tog, 1 hdc in each st ending 1 hdc in tch, turn.
Rep the last 2 rows 1 (1:1:2) more times, then the first (first:first:0) row again. 8 (9:10:11) sts. Work 1 (1:1:2) rows. Fasten off.

RIGHT FRONT

Work as given for Left Front (patt is reversible.)

SLEEVES

Using larger hook and 2 strands of yarn tog, ch 23 (25:27:29).
Foundation row Work as given for Back. 22 (24:26:28) sts.
Row 1 As given for Back.
Cont in patt, inc 1 st at each end of the 3rd (4th:4th:5th) row and 4 foll 4th (5th:6th:6th) rows. 32 (34:36:38) sts.
Cont straight until sleeve measures 9½ (11½:13: 14½) in. (24 [29:33:37] cm). Fasten off.

POCKETS (MAKE 2)

Using larger hook and 2 strands of yarn tog, ch 9 (9:9:10).
Foundation row As given for Back. 8 (8:8:9) sts.
Row 1 Work as given for Back.
Cont in patt until pocket measures 3 (3:3:3½) in. (8 [8:8:9] cm). Change to smaller hook.
Next row Ch 1 (counts as 1 sc), 1 sc in each st ending 1 sc in tch.
Work 1 more row in sc. Fasten off.

COLLAR

Join shoulders.
Row 1 With RS facing and using larger hook and 2 strands of yarn tog, join yarn at neck edge on Right Front. Ch 2 (counts as 1 hdc), work 12 (13:13:14) hdc up right neck, 22 (23:24:25) hdc along back of neck, and 13 (14:14:15) hdc down left neck, turn. 48 (51:52:55) sts.
Row 2 Ch 2 (counts as 1 hdc) 1 hdc in each st ending 1 hdc in tch, turn.
Rep Row 2 until collar measures 2 (2:2:2½) in. (5 [5:5:6] cm). Fasten off.

FINISHING

Mark positions 5¼ (5½:6:6¼) in. (13.5 [14:15:16] cm) down from each side of shoulder seams. Fold sleeves in half lengthwise and place center point at shoulder seam. Sew sleeve tops between markers, then join side and sleeve seams. Weave in all yarn ends.

Edges

With RS facing and using smaller hook and 2 strands of yarn tog, join yarn at right side seam.
Round 1 Ch 1 (counts as 1 sc), work in sc evenly all around edges, working 2 sc into each corner on lower fronts and each corner on collar, ss to 1 ch at beg, turn. Work 1 more round in sc, working 2 sc in each corner, ss to 1 ch at beg. Fasten off. Weave in yarn ends.

Cuffs

With RS facing and using smaller hook and 2 strands of yarn tog, join yarn at sleeve seam.
Round 1 Ch 1 (counts as 1 sc), work in sc evenly around cuff edge, ss to 1 ch at beg, turn.
Work 1 more round in sc. Fasten off.
Position a pocket on the center of each front, 1½ in. (4 cm) up from lower edge, and sew neatly in place.

Using sewing thread, sew zipper neatly in position along front and collar edges.
Weave in yarn ends.

Rag Doll

Make a little girl happy with this soft and cuddly doll, dressed in a pretty frilly dress. The doll is made in rounds (of simple single crochet), so there are no seams to sew up, and her clothes require just double and single crochet stitches.

Skill level: INTERMEDIATE

MEASUREMENTS

Completed doll measures 15¾ in. (40 cm) tall.

MATERIALS

- Sirdar Country Style 4ply: 1 x 100 g (3½ oz.) ball in each of cream 411 (A), lilac 531 (B), pink 526 (C), pale yellow 535 (D)

- C/2 (2.50 mm) crochet hook

- Washable toy stuffing

- 1 button (for dress), ⅜ in. (1 cm) in diameter

- Small amounts of embroidery thread in blue and red

- Large crewel or chenille needle

GAUGE

24 stitches and 28½ rows to 4 in. (10 cm) measured over single crochet fabric on C/2 (2.50 mm) hook. Change hook size, if necessary, to achieve this gauge

ABBREVIATIONS

dc2tog—[*yoh and insert hook as indicated, yoh and draw loop through, yoh and draw through 2 loops] twice, yoh and draw through all 3 loops on hook.
dc3tog—[*yoh and insert hook as indicated, yoh and draw loop through, yoh and draw through 2 loops] 3 times, yoh and draw through all 3 loops on hook.
sc2tog—[insert hook as indicated, yoh and draw loop through] twice, yoh and draw through all 3 loops.
See also page 11.

DOLL

ARMS (make 2)

Using A, ch 3 and join with a ss to form a ring.
Round 1 (RS) Ch 1 (does not count as st), 5 sc into ring, ss to first sc, turn. 5 sts.
Round 2 Ch 1 (does not count as st), 2 sc into each sc to end, ss to first sc, turn. 10 sts.
Round 3 Ch 1 (does not count as st), [1 sc into next sc, 2 sc into next sc] 5 times, ss to first sc, turn. 15 sts.
Round 4 Ch 1 (does not count as st), 1 sc into each sc to end, ss to first sc, turn.
Round 5 As Round 4.
Round 6 Ch 1 (does not count as st), [2 sc into next sc, 1 sc into each of next 2 sc] 5 times, ss to first sc, turn. 20 sts.
Rounds 7–10 As Round 4.
Round 11 Ch 1 (does not count as st), [sc2tog over next 2 sc] 10 times, ss to first sc2tog, turn. 10 sts.
Round 12 As Round 3. 15 sts.
Rounds 13–30 As Round 4.
  Fasten off. Weave in all yarn ends.

FIRST LEG

Using A, ch 3 and join with a ss to form a ring.
Round 1 (RS) Ch 1 (does not count as st), 5 sc into ring, ss to first sc, turn. 5 sts.
Round 2 Ch 1 (does not count as st), 2 sc into each sc to end, ss to first sc, turn. 10 sts.
Round 3 Ch 1 (does not count as st), [1 sc into next sc, 2 sc into next sc] 5 times, ss to first sc, turn. 15 sts.

Round 4 Ch 1 (does not count as st), 1 sc into each sc to end, ss to first sc, turn.

Round 5 As Round 4.

Round 6 Ch 1 (does not count as st), [2 sc into next sc, 1 sc into each of next 2 sc] 5 times, ss to first sc, turn. 20 sts.

Round 7 Ch 1 (does not count as st), [2 sc into next sc, 1 sc into each of next 3 sc] 5 times, ss to first sc, turn. 25 sts.

Rounds 8–11 As Round 4.

Round 12 Ch 1 (does not count as st), 1 sc into first sc, [sc2tog over next 2 sc] 12 times, ss to first sc, turn. 13 sts.

Round 13 Ch 1 (does not count as st), [2 sc into next st, 1 sc into next st] 6 times, 2 sc into last st, ss to first sc, turn. 20 sts.

Rounds 14–42 As Round 4.

Fasten off.

SECOND LEG

Work as given for First Leg to end of Round 42.

Do not fasten off.

BODY

Using A join Legs to form Body as follows:

Round 43 (RS) Ch 1 (does not count as st), 1 sc into each sc of Second Leg, starting on last sc of Round 42 of First Leg, 1 sc into each of the 20 sc of First Leg, then ss to first sc, turn. 40 sts.

Rounds 44–52 As Round 4.

Insert toy stuffing into Legs and lower part of Body.

Shape waist

Round 53 Ch 1 (does not count as st), [sc2tog over next 2 sc] 20 times, ss to first sc, turn. 20 sts.

Round 54 Ch 1 (does not count as st), 2 sc into each sc to end, ss to first sc, turn. 40 sts.

Rounds 55–64 As Round 4.

Join arms to body

Round 65 (RS) Ch 1 (does not count as st), 1 sc into each of first 10 sc, starting on first sc of one Arm 1 sc into each of 15 sc of first Arm, 1 sc into each of next 20 sc of Body, starting on first sc of second Arm 1 sc into each of 15 sc of second Arm, 1 sc into rem 10 sc

of Body, ss to first sc, turn. 70 sts.

Round 66 Ch 1 (does not count as st), 1 sc into each of first 8 sc, *sc2tog over next 2 sc, 1 sc into each of next 5 sc, sc2tog over next 2 sc, 1 sc into next sc, sc2tog over next 2 sc, 1 sc into each of next 5 sc, sc2tog over next 2 sc*, 1 sc into each of next 16 sc, rep from * to * once more, 1 sc into each of last 8 sc, ss to first sc, turn. 62 sts.

Round 67 As Round 4.

Insert toy stuffing into Arms and upper part of Body.

Round 68 Ch 1 (does not count as st), 1 sc into each of first 7 sc, *sc2tog over next 2 sc, 1 sc into each of next 4 sc, sc2tog over next 2 sc, 1 sc into next sc, sc2tog over next 2 sc, 1 sc into each of next 4 sc, sc2tog over next 2 sc*, 1 sc into each of next 14 sc, rep from * to * once more, 1 sc into each of last 7 sc, ss to first sc, turn. 54 sts.

Round 69 As Round 4.

Round 70 Ch 1 (does not count as st), 1 sc into each of first 6 sc, *sc2tog over next 2 sc, 1 sc into each of next 3 sc, sc2tog over next 2 sc, 1 sc into next sc, sc2tog over next 2 sc, 1 sc into each of next 3 sc, sc2tog over next 2 sc*, 1 sc into each of next 12 sc, rep from * to * once more, 1 sc into each of last 6 sc, ss to first sc, turn. 46 sts.

Round 71 As Round 4.

Round 72 Ch 1 (does not count as st), 1 sc into each of first 5 sc, *sc2tog over next 2 sc, 1 sc into each of next 2 sc, sc2tog over next 2 sc, 1 sc into next sc, sc2tog over next 2 sc, 1 sc into each of next 2 sc, sc2tog over next 2 sc*, 1 sc into each of next 10 sc, rep from * to * once more, 1 sc into each of last 5 sc, ss to first sc, turn. 38 sts.

Round 73 As Round 4.

Round 74 Ch 1 (does not count as st), 1 sc into each of first 4 sc, *sc2tog over next 2 sc, [1 sc into next sc, sc2tog over next 2 sc] 3 times*, 1 sc into each of next 8 sc, rep from * to * once more, 1 sc into each of last 4 sc, ss to first sc, turn. 30 sts.

Round 75 As Round 4.

Shape neck and head

Round 76 Ch 1 (does not count as st), [sc2tog over next 2 sc] 15 times, ss to first sc2tog, turn. 15 sts.

Round 77 As Round 4.

Insert toy stuffing into upper part of Body.

Round 78 Ch 1 (does not count as st), 2 sc into each sc to end, ss to first sc, turn. 30 sts.

Round 79 As Round 4.

Round 80 Ch 1 (does not count as st), [2 sc into next sc, 1 sc into each of next 4 sc] 6 times, ss to first sc, turn. 36 sts.

Round 81 As Round 4.

Round 82 Ch 1 (does not count as st), [2 sc into next sc, 1 sc into each of next 5 sc] 6 times, ss to first sc, turn. 42 sts.

Round 83 As Round 4.

Round 84 Ch 1 (does not count as st), [2 sc into next sc, 1 sc into each of next 6 sc] 6 times, ss to first sc, turn. 48 sts.

Rounds 85–93 As Round 4.

Round 94 Ch 1 (does not count as st), [1 sc into each of next 6 sc, sc2tog over next 2 sc] 6 times, ss to first sc2tog, turn. 42 sts.

Round 95 As Round 4.

Round 96 Ch 1 (does not count as st), [1 sc into each of next 5 sc, sc2tog over next 2 sc] 6 times, ss to first sc2tog, turn. 36 sts.

Insert toy filling into neck and Head.

Round 97 Ch 1 (does not count as st), [1 sc into each of next 4 sc, sc2tog over next 2 sc] 6 times, ss to first sc2tog, turn. 30 sts.

Round 98 Ch 1 (does not count as st), [1 sc into each of next 3 sc, sc2tog over next 2 sc] 6 times, ss to first sc, turn. 24 sts.

Round 99 Ch 1 (does not count as st), [sc2tog over next 2 sc] 12 times, ss to first sc2tog. 12 sts.

Round 100 Ch 1 (does not count as st), [sc2tog over next 2 sc] 6 times, ss to first sc2tog. 6 sts.

Fasten off.

Attaching hair to head

Cut D into 20-in. (40-cm) lengths. Attach to head by working a line of chain stitch, using crewel or chenille needle and D, through head, from back neck to top of forehead, catching center of yarn lengths under stitches. Using a length of B, tie hair in bunches at sides of head, finishing with a bow.

Embroider features

Using blue embroidery thread, embroider eyes by working a few small straight stitches. Using red embroidery thread, embroider mouth in satin stitch. For nose, work a tiny satin stitch block using cream yarn.

PANTIES

FIRST LEG

Using B, ch 24 and join with a ss to form a ring.

Round 1 (RS) Ch 3 (counts as first dc), skip ch where ss was worked, 2 dc into next ch, [1 dc into next ch, 2 dc into next ch] 11 times, ss to top of 3 ch at beg of round. 36 sts.

Round 2 3 ch (counts as first dc), skip st at base of 3 ch, 1 dc into each dc to end, ss to top of 3 ch at beg of round.

Round 3 As Round 2.

Fasten off.

SECOND LEG

Work as given for First Leg to end of Round 3.

Do not fasten off.

MAIN SECTION

Join Legs as follows:

Round 4 (RS) Ss into same place as ss at end of round 3 of First Leg, ch 3 (counts as first dc), skip st at base of 3 ch, 1 dc into each of next 35 dc of First Leg, starting on first dc of Round 3 of Second Leg, 1 dc into each of the 36 sts of Second Leg, then ss to top of 3 ch at beg of round. 72 sts.

Rounds 5–10 As Round 2.

Round 11 Ch 3 (counts as first dc), skip dc at base of 3 ch, dc2tog over next 2 dc, *1 dc into next dc, dc2tog over next 2 dc, rep from * to end, ss to top of 3 ch at beg of round. 48 sts.

WAISTBAND

Round 12 Ch 1 (does not count as st), 1 sc into each st to end, ss to first sc, turn.

Rounds 13 and 14 As Round 12.

Fasten off.

LEG RUFFLES (make 2)

With RS facing, using C, rejoin yarn to one Leg foundation ch edge and cont as follows:

Round 1 Ch 1 (does not count as st), 1 sc into each foundation ch to end, ss to first sc. 24 sts.

Round 2 Ch 4 (counts as 1 dc and 1 ch), 1 dc into sc at base of 4 ch, ch 1, *(1 dc, ch 1 and 1 dc) into next sc, ch 1, rep from * to end, ss to 3rd of 4 ch at beg of round.

Round 3 Ss into first ch sp, ch 1 (does not count as st), 1 sc into first ch sp, ch 3, *1 sc into next ch sp, ch 3, rep from * to end, ss to first sc.

Fasten off.

Using B, ch 100 and fasten off. Thread this ch through waistband and tie in bow at center front.

DRESS

SKIRT

Using B, ch 144 and join with a ss to form a ring.

Round 1 (RS) ch 3 (counts as first dc), skip ch where ss was worked, 1 dc into each ch to end, ss to top of 3 ch at beg of round. 144 sts.

Round 2 Ch 3 (counts as first dc), skip st at base of 3 ch, 1 dc into each dc to end, ss to top of 3 ch at beg of round.

Rounds 3–17 As Round 2.

Round 18 Ch 3 (does not count as st), skip st at base of 3 ch, dc2tog over next 2 dc, [dc3tog over next 3 dc] 47 times, ss to top of dc2tog at beg of round. 48 sts.

Bodice

Round 19 Ch 1 (does not count as st), 1 sc into each st to end, ss to first sc, turn.

This round forms sc fabric.

Rounds 20–24 As Round 19.

Divide for armholes and back opening

Row 25 Ch 1 (does not count as st), 1 sc into each of first 11 sc, turn, leaving rem sts unworked.

Work on this set of 11 sts only for left back.

Row 26 Ch 1 (does not count as st), sc2tog over first 2 sc—1 st decreased, 1 sc into each sc to end, turn. 10 sts.

Row 27 Ch 1 (does not count as st), 1 sc into each of first 8 sc, sc2tog over last 2 sts—1 st decreased, turn. 9 sts.

Work another 13 rows.

Fasten off.

Shape front

Return to last complete round worked, skip 2 sc after left back, rejoin yarn to next sc and cont as follows:

Row 25 Ch 1 (does not count as st), 1 sc into each of next 22 sc, turn, leaving rem sts unworked.

Work in sc fabric on this set of 22 sts only for front.

Dec 1 st at each end of next 2 rows. 18 sts.

Work 8 rows.

Shape neck

Row 36 Ch 1 (does not count as st), 1 sc into each of first 7 sc, turn, leaving rem sts unworked.

Dec 1 st at neck edge of next 2 rows. 5 sts.

Work 2 rows.

Fasten off.

Return to last complete row worked on front, skip center 4 sc, rejoin yarn to next sc, ch 1 (does not count as st), 1 sc into each sc to end, turn. 7 sts. Complete second side of front neck to match first.

Shape right back

Return to last complete round worked, skip 2 sc after front, rejoin yarn to next sc, ch 1 (does NOT count as st), 1 sc into each sc to end, turn. 11 sts. Complete to match Left Back.

SLEEVES

Using B, ch 18 and join with a ss to form a ring.

Round 1 (RS) Ch 3 (counts as first dc), 1 dc into same place as ss, 2 dc into each ch to end, ss to top of 3 ch at beg of round. 36 sts.

Round 2 Ch 3 (counts as first dc), skip st at base of 3 ch, 1 dc into each dc to end, ss to top of 3 ch at beg of round.

Round 3 As Round 2.

Round 4 Ch 1 (does not count as st), 1 sc into each of first 2 dc, 1 hdc into next dc, 1 dc into each of next 30 dc, 1 hdc into next dc, 1 sc into each of last 2 dc, ss to first sc.

Round 5 Ch 1 (does not count as st), 1 sc into each of first 4 sts, 1 hdc into next dc, 1 dc into each of next 26 dc, 1 hdc into next dc, 1 sc into each of last 4 sts, ss to first sc.

Round 6 Ch 1 (does not count as st), 1 sc into each of first 6 sts, 1 hdc into next dc, 1 dc into each of next 22 dc, 1 hdc into next dc, 1 sc into each of last 6 sts, ss to first sc.

Round 7 Ch 1 (does not count as st), 1 sc into each of first 8 sts, 1 hdc into next dc, [dc2tog over next 2 dc] 9 times, 1 hdc into next dc, 1 sc into each of last 8 sts, ss to first sc.

Fasten off.

FINISHING

Join shoulder seams. Sew sleeves into armholes, easing in fullness.

Neck edging

With RS facing, using D, attach yarn at top of left back opening edge and work one row of sc evenly around neck edge.

Fasten off.

Ruffles

Using C, work Ruffles around lower edge of Sleeves and Skirt as given for Panty Leg Ruffles.

Make button loop and attach button to fasten back neck.

The doll's hair is made by cutting lengths of pale yellow yarn and then stitching them from the back neck to the top of the forehead.

HOME ACCESSORIES

Fill your home with gorgeous crochet items—from pretty little table toppers to colorful afghans in jewel-bright yarns. The range of yarns available means that you can add your own personal touch to any room.

Rag Rug

Use up scraps of printed or plain cotton fabric to create a colorful rug that can handle wear but is pretty too. Ideal to use as either a bath mat, bedside rug, or doormat, it can go into the washing machine as often as necessary!

★
Skill level: BEGINNER

MEASUREMENTS

27 × 21 in.
68 × 53 cm

MATERIALS

- approx. 6½ yds. (6 m) of 45-in. (115-cm) wide printed cotton fabric, cut into ½–⅝-in. (12–15-mm) wide bias strips (see Note, below)

- N/15 (10.00 mm) crochet hook

GAUGE

8 stitches and 7½ rows to 4 in. (10 cm) measured over single crochet fabric using N/15 (10.00 mm) hook. Change hook size, if necessary, to obtain this gauge.

ABBREVIATIONS

See page 11.

NOTE

The rug is crocheted from bias strips of printed cotton fabric. Trim selvage from fabrics, then cut fabrics into ½–⅝-in. (12–15-mm) wide bias strips. If using different fabric prints, mix all the strips together so that the end result will mix all the different prints together. You can also use each fabric separately to create soft bands of color. As you work, join strips by overlapping ends of strips and working one sc using both strips. Leave ¾–2½-in. (2–6-cm) ends of strips free on RS of work.

RUG

Using first bias strip, ch 15.

Foundation round (WS) 3 sc into 2nd ch from hook, 1 sc into each of next 12 ch, 6 sc into last ch, working back along other side of foundation ch work 1 sc into each of next 12 ch, 3 sc into last ch (this is same ch as used for 3 sc at beg of round, ss to first sc, turn. 36 sts. Cont as follows:

Round 1 (RS) Ch 1 (does not count as st), 1 sc into first sc, 3 sc into next (corner) sc, 1 sc into each of next 14 sc, 3 sc into next (corner) sc, 1 sc into each of next 2 sc, 3 sc into next (corner) sc, 1 sc into each of next 14 sc, 3 sc into next (corner) sc, 1 sc into last sc, ss to first sc, turn. 44 sts.

Round 2 Ch 1 (does not count as st), 1 sc into each of first 2 sc, 3 sc into next (corner) sc, 1 sc into each of next 16 sc, 3 sc into next (corner) sc, 1 sc into each of next 4 sc, 3 sc into next (corner) sc, 1 sc into each of next 16 sc, 3 sc into next (corner) sc, 1 sc into each of last 2 sc, ss to first sc, turn. 52 sts.

Round 3 Ch 1 (does not count as st), 1 sc into each of first 3 sc, 3 sc into next (corner) sc, 1 sc into each of next 18 sc, 3 sc into next (corner) sc, 1 sc into each of next 6 sc, 3 sc into next (corner) sc, 1 sc into each of next 18 sc, 3 sc into next (corner) sc, 1 sc into each of last 3 sc, ss to first sc, turn. 60 sts.

Round 4 Ch 1 (does not count as st), 1 sc into each of first 4 sc, 3 sc into next (corner) sc, 1 sc into each of next 20 sc, 3 sc into next (corner) sc, 1 sc into each of next 8 sc, 3 sc into next (corner) sc, 1 sc into each of next 20 sc, 3 sc into next (corner) sc, 1 sc into each of last 4 sc, ss to first sc, turn. 68 sts.

Round 5 Ch 1 (does not count as st), 1 sc into each of first 5 sc, 3 sc into next (corner) sc, 1 sc into each of next 22 sc, 3 sc into next (corner) sc, 1 sc into each of next 10 sc, 3 sc into next (corner) sc, 1 sc into each of next 22 sc, 3 sc into next (corner) sc, 1 sc into each of last 5 sc, ss to first sc, turn. 76 sts.

Round 6 Ch 1 (does not count as st), *1 sc into each sc to corner sc, 3 sc into next (corner) sc, rep from * 3 more times, 1 sc into each sc to end, ss to first sc, turn.

Rep Round 6 until all fabric strips have been used up. Fasten off.

FINISHING

Press carefully, using a warm iron over a damp cloth. Trim free ends on RS of rug so that all ends are approximately ¾–1½ in. (2–4 cm) long.

Patchwork Cover-up

Create a modern heirloom with a bedspread that gives a new twist to the classic look of patchwork. Worked in neutral shades of fine pure cotton yarn, each square is made in the same way—it's just the size that changes!

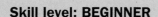

Skill level: BEGINNER

MEASUREMENTS

89 × 89 in.
225 × 225 cm

MATERIALS

- 36 × 50 g (1¾ oz.) balls of Rowan Cotton Glacé in Oyster 730 (A)

- 28 × 50 g (1¾ oz.) balls of Rowan Cotton Glacé in Ecru 725 (B)

- 29 × 50 g (1¾ oz.) balls of Rowan Cotton Glacé in Bleached 726 (C)

- D/3 (3.25 mm) crochet hook

GAUGE

Small Motif measures 4 in. (10 cm) square using D/3 (3.25 mm) crochet hook. Change hook size, if necessary, to obtain this gauge.

ABBREVIATIONS

See page 11.

NOTE

The bedspread is made of 48 Small Motifs (15 in A, 16 in B, and 17 in C); 89 Medium Motifs (32 in A, 29 in B, and 28 in C); and 5 Large Motifs (2 in A, 1 in B, and 2 in C).

BEDSPREAD

SMALL MOTIF

Ch 4 and join with a ss to form a ring.

Round 1 (RS) Ch 3 (counts as first dc), 2 dc into ring, (ch 2, 3 dc into ring) 3 times, 1 hdc into top of 3 ch at beg of round.

Round 2 Ss into first ch sp—this is sp formed by hdc at end of previous round, ch 3 (counts as first dc), (2 dc, ch 2, and 3 dc) into same corner ch sp, *ch 1, (3 dc, ch 2, and 3 dc) into next corner ch sp, rep from * twice more, 1 sc into top of 3 ch at beg of round.

Round 3 Ss into first ch sp—this is sp formed by sc at end of previous round, ch 3 (counts as first dc), 2 dc into same ch sp, *ch 1, (3 dc, ch 2, and 3 dc) into next corner ch sp**, ch 1, 3 dc into next ch sp, rep from * to end, ending last rep at **, 1 sc into top of 3 ch at beg of round.

Round 4 Ss into first ch sp—this is sp formed by sc at end of previous round, ch 3 (counts as first dc), 2 dc into same ch sp, *ch 1, 3 dc into next ch sp, ch 1, (3 dc, ch 2 and 3 dc) into next corner ch sp**, ch 1, 3 dc into next ch sp, rep from * to end, ending last rep at **, 1 sc into top of 3 ch at beg of round.

Round 5 Ss into first ch sp—this is sp formed by sc at end of previous round, ch 3 (counts as first dc), 2 dc into same ch sp, *(ch 1, 3 dc into next ch sp) twice, ch 1, (3 dc, ch 2, and 3 dc) into next corner ch sp, ch 1**, 3 dc into next ch sp, rep from * to end, ending last rep at **, 1 ss into top of 3 ch at beg of round.

Fasten off. Weave in yarn ends.

Small Motif should be 4 in. (10 cm) square; adjust hook size now, if necessary.

In each corner of motif, there is a 2-ch sp, and along sides of motif between these ch sps there are 5 groups of 3 dc, each group separated by 1 ch.

MEDIUM MOTIF

Work as for Small Motif to end of Round 4.

Round 5 Ss into first ch sp—this is sp formed by sc at end of previous round, ch 3 (counts as first dc), 2 dc into same ch sp, *(ch 1, 3 dc into next ch sp) twice, ch 1, (3 dc, ch 2, and 3 dc) into next corner ch sp**, ch 1, 3 dc into next ch sp, rep from * to end, ending last rep at **, 1 sc into top of 3 ch at beg of round.

Round 6 Ss into first ch sp—this is sp formed by sc at end of previous round, ch 3 (counts as first dc), 2 dc into same ch sp, *ch 1, 3 dc into next ch sp, rep from * to end, working (3 dc, ch 2, and 3 dc) into each of the 4 corner ch sps, 1 sc into top of 3 ch at beg of round.

Rep Round 6 until Medium Motif measures 8 in. (20 cm) square, replacing the (1 sc into top of 3 ch at beg of round) at end of last round with (ch 1, ss to top of 3 ch at beg of round).

Fasten off. Weave in yarn ends.

LARGE MOTIF

Work as for Medium Motif until this Motif measures 16 in. (40 cm) square, replacing the (1 sc into top of 3 ch at beg of round) at end of last round with (ch 1, ss to top of 3 ch at beg of round).

Fasten off. Weave in yarn ends.

ASSEMBLING BEDSPREAD

Following diagram, join motifs to form one large square using A. Join motifs by working a row of sc along edges, holding motifs with right sides facing and working each sc through edges of both motifs.

Edging

With RS facing and using A, rejoin yarn to outer edge of joined motifs and work one round of sc evenly around entire outer edge, working 3 sc into corners and ending with ss to first sc.

☐ small motif

☐ medium motif

☐ large motif

Round 1 Ch 1 (does NOT count as st), 1 sc into each st to end, working 3 sc into corners and ending with ss to first sc.

Fasten off A and join in B.

Round 2 Ch 3 (counts as first dc), 1 dc into each sc to end, working 5 dc into corners and ending with ss to top of 3 ch at beg of round.

Fasten off B and join in C.

Rounds 3 and 4 As Round 1 but using C.

Fasten off. Weave in all yarn ends.

FINISHING

Press carefully, following instructions on yarn label.

Rainbow Lap Throw

Create a shimmering rainbow of color to keep you cozy on cool evenings! This throw uses an easy-care microfiber yarn in strong, jewel-like colors to produce a dazzling effect.

 ★★★

Skill level: ADVANCED

MEASUREMENTS

52 × 61 in. (132 × 152 cm)

MATERIALS

- 4 × 70 g (2½ oz.) balls of Lion Brand Micro Spun in each of the following: Cherry Red 113 (A), Mango 186 (B), Buttercup 158 (C), Lime 194 (D), Turquoise 148 (E), Royal Blue 109 (F), and Purple 147 (G)

- G/6 (4.25 mm) crochet hook

GAUGE

15½ stitches and 24 rows to 4 in. (10 cm) measured over pattern, using G/6 (4.25 mm) hook. Change hook size, if necessary, to obtain this gauge.

ABBREVIATIONS

Sp6 (5:4:3:2)—work a sc into next st 5 (4:3:2:1) rows below next sc and draw up loop to enclose work—take care st is left loose enough that work does not pucker.
See also page 11.

MAIN SECTION

Using A, ch 201.

Foundation row (WS) 1 sc into 2nd ch from hook, 1 sc into each ch to end, turn. 200 sts.

Next row Ch 1 (does not count as st), 1 sc into each sc to end, turn.

Rep last row 3 more times.

Cont in patt as follows:

Break off A and join in B.

Row 1 (RS) Ch 1 (does not count as st), 1 sc into first sc, *Sp6, Sp5, Sp4, Sp3, Sp2, 1 sc into next sc, rep from * to last sc, 1 sc into last sc, turn.

Rows 2–6 Ch 1 (does not count as st), 1 sc into each sc to end, turn.

Break off B and join in C.

Row 7 (RS) Ch 1 (does not count as st), 1 sc into first sc, *1 sc into next sc, Sp2, Sp3, Sp4, Sp5, Sp6, rep from * to last sc, 1 sc into last sc, turn.

Rows 8–12 Ch 1 (does not count as st), 1 sc into each sc to end, turn.

These 12 rows form patt.

Joining in and breaking off colors as required, cont in patt in stripes as follows:

Using D, work 6 rows.

Using E, work 6 rows.

Using F, work 6 rows.

Using G, work 6 rows.

Using A, work 6 rows.

Last 42 rows form stripe sequence.

Keeping patt and stripes correct, cont as set until 60 stripes in total (including first 5 rows in A) have been worked, ending with 6 rows using D. (Main Section should measure approximately 59 in. [150 cm].)

Using E, work 1 row, thus ending after 7th patt row and with a RS row—do not turn at end of this row.

Do not fasten off.

BORDER

With RS facing and using E, work around entire outer edge of Main Section as follows: 2 more sc into same st as last sc of last row of Main Section, work in sc evenly down row-end edge to foundation ch edge, 3 sc into first ch across base of foundation ch edge, 1 sc into each foundation ch to end, work another 2 sc into last ch of foundation ch edge, then work in sc up other row-end edge to top of last row of Main Section, then work another 2 sc into same place as sc at beg of last row of Main Section, ss to sc at beg of last row of Main Section, turn.

Next round (WS) Ch 1 (does not count as st), 1 sc into each sc to end, working 3 sc into each corner sc and ending with ss to first sc, turn.

Break off E and join in C.

Rep last round once more.

Fasten off. Weave in yarn ends.

FINISHING

Press carefully, following instructions on yarn label.

The simple single crochet border adds just the right finishing touch.

Chevron Throw

Light and airy—yet warm and cuddly—this stunning throw is designed to keep you snug on long, cold winter nights. It is easily made in stripes of high- and low-textured yarns.

Skill level: INTERMEDIATE

MEASUREMENTS

53 × 60 in. (135 × 152 cm)—excluding tassels

MATERIALS

- 7 × 50 g (1¾ oz.) balls of Sirdar Country Style DK in Raspberry 539 (A)

- 16 × 50 g (1¾ oz.) balls of Sirdar Funky Fur in Gemstone 540 (B)

- H/8 (5.00 mm) crochet hook

GAUGE

2 patt repeats (24 sts) and 8 rows to 6 in. (15 cm) measured over patt using H/8 (5.00 mm) crochet hook. Change hook size, if necessary, to obtain this gauge.

ABBREVIATIONS

dc5tog—*yoh and insert hook into next st, yoh and draw loop through, yoh and draw through 2 loops, rep from * 4 more times, yoh and draw through all 6 loops on hook. *See also page 11.*

dc5tog   chain stitch

double crochet

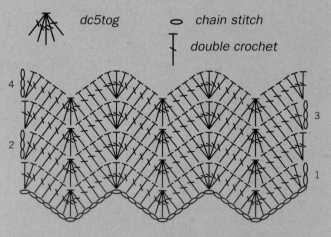

THROW

Using A, ch 219.

Foundation row (RS): 2 dc into 3rd ch from hook, *1 dc into each of next 3 ch, dc5tog over next 5 ch, 1 dc into each of next 3 ch**, 5 dc into next ch, rep from * to end, ending last rep at **, 3 dc into last ch, turn. 217 sts, 18 patt reps.

Cont in patt as follows:

Row 1: Using A, ch 3 (counts as first dc), 2 dc into dc at base of 3 ch, *1 dc into each of next 3 dc, dc5tog over next 5 sts, 1 dc into each of next 3 dc**, 5 dc into next dc, rep from * to end, ending last rep at **, 3 dc into top of 3 ch at beg of previous row, turn.

Join in B.

Rows 2 and 3: Using B, as Row 1.

Row 4: As Row 1.

These 4 rows form patt.

Work in patt for another 77 rows, ending after 2 rows using A and a WS row. Work should measure approx. 60 in (152 cm).

Fasten off.

FINISHING

Do not press.

For each tassel, cut 20 lengths of A, each 12 in. (30 cm) long. Cut another length of A and tie first 20 lengths together at center. Fold lengths in half at point where they are tied together, and bind lengths together approx ¾ in. (2 cm) from fold to form tassel. Make another 36 tassels in this way and attach one tassel to each "point" along shorter edges of throw.

Looped Pillows and Rug

Add a touch of luxury and warmth to your home with these shaggy pillows and matching rug. The yarn is hand-dyed pure wool, which means you'll end up with your very own designer originals.

MEASUREMENTS

Rug
23½ × 38 in.
60 × 97 cm

Square pillow
18 × 18 in.
45 × 45 cm

Round pillow
18 in. (45 cm) in diameter

MATERIALS

- Colinette Graffiti: 13 × 100 g (3½ oz.) hanks in Neptune 139 (Rug), 7 × 100 g (3½ oz.) hanks in Magenta 94 (Square Pillow), and 6 × 100 g (3½ oz.) hanks in Magenta 94 (Round Pillow)

- K/10½ (7.00 mm) crochet hook

- 18-in. (45-cm) square pillow form

- 18-in. (45-cm) diameter round pillow form

NOTE
The exact amount of yarn required will depend on the length of the loops. Yarn quantities given are the amounts used for the photographed items. If your loops are slightly longer, you may need slightly more yarn. Similarly, if they are slightly shorter, you may have yarn left over.

GAUGE

10 stitches and 10 rows to 4 in. (10 cm) measured over pattern using K/10½ (7.00 mm) hook. Change hook size, if necessary, to obtain this gauge.

ABBREVIATIONS

dc2tog—[insert hook as indicated, yoh, and draw loop through] twice, yoh and draw through all 3 loops on hook
loop 1—insert hook into next st, using finger of left hand draw out yarn to form a loop approx 2–2½ in. (5–6 cm) long, pick up both strands of this loop with hook and draw through st, yoh, and draw loop through all 3 loops on hook.
See also page 11.

SQUARE PILLOW

FRONT

Ch 46.

Foundation row (RS) 1 sc into 2nd ch from hook, 1 sc into each ch to end, turn. 45 sts.

Cont in patt as follows:

Row 1 (WS) Ch 1 (does not count as st), 1 sc into first sc, loop 1 into each sc to last sc, 1 sc into last sc, turn.

Row 2 Ch 1 (does not count as st), 1 sc into each st to end, turn.

These 2 rows form patt.

Cont in patt for another 42 rows, ending after a RS row.

Fasten off. Weave in yarn ends.

BACK

Ch 46.

Foundation row (RS) 1 sc into 2nd ch from hook, 1 sc into each ch to end, turn. 45 sts.

Cont in sc fabric as follows:

Row 1 (WS) Ch 1 (does not count as st), 1 sc into each sc to end, turn.

This row forms sc fabric.

Cont in sc fabric for another 43 rows, ending with a RS row. Fasten off. Weave in yarn ends.

FINISHING

Do not press. Join Front to Back along 3 edges. Insert pillow form and sew fourth side closed. Weave in yarn ends. Carefully cut each loop to form furry effect.

ROUND PILLOW

FRONT

Ch 22.

Foundation row (RS) 1 sc into 2nd ch from hook, 1 sc into each ch to end, turn. 21 sts.

Cont in patt as follows:

Row 1 (WS) Ch 1 (does not count as st), [1 sc and loop 1] into first sc—1 st increased, loop 1 into each sc to last sc, [loop 1 and 1 sc] into last sc—1 st increased, turn. 23 sts.

Row 2 Ch 1 (does NOT count as st), 2 sc into first sc—

1 st increased, 1 sc into each st to last sc, 2 sc into last sc—1 st increased, turn. 25 sts.

These 2 rows form patt and start shaping.

Working all increases as now set, cont in patt, inc 1 st at each end of next 7 rows, then on foll alt row, then on foll 3rd row, then on foll 4th row. 45 sts.

Work 8 rows, ending after a RS row.

Row 27 (WS) Ch 1 (does NOT count as st), sc2tog over first 2 sts—1 st decreased, patt to last 2 sts, sc2tog over last 2 sts—1 st decreased, turn. 43 sts.

Working all decreases as set by last row, dec 1 st at each end of 4th and foll 3rd row, then on foll alt row, then on foll 8 rows, ending with a RS row. 21 sts.

Fasten off. Weave in yarn ends.

BACK

Ch 22.

Foundation row (RS) 1 sc into 2nd ch from hook, 1 sc into each ch to end, turn. 21 sts.

Cont in sc fabric as follows:

Row 1 (WS) Ch 1 (does NOT count as st), 2 sc into first sc—1 st increased, 1 sc into each sc to last sc, 2 sc into last sc—1 st increased, turn. 23 sts.

This row forms sc fabric and starts shaping.

Working all increases as set by last row, cont in sc fabric, inc 1 st at each end of next 8 rows, then on foll alt row, then on foll 3rd row, then on foll 4th row. 45 sts.

Work 8 rows, ending with a RS row.

Row 27 (WS) Ch 1 (does NOT count as st), sc2tog over first 2 sts—1 st decreased, 1 sc into each sc to last 2 sts, sc2tog over last 2 sts—1 st decreased, turn. 43 sts.

Working all decreases as set by last row, dec 1 st at each end of 4th and foll 3rd row, then on foll alt row, then on foll 8 rows, ending after a RS row. 21 sts.

Fasten off.

FINISHING

Do not press. Join Front to Back, leaving an opening for inserting pillow form. Insert pillow form and sew opening closed. Weave in yarn ends. Carefully cut each loop to form furry effect.

RUG

Ch 61.

Foundation row (RS) 1 sc into 2nd ch from hook, 1 sc into each ch to end, turn. 60 sts.

Cont in patt as follows:

Row 1 (WS) Ch 1 (does not count as st), 1 dc into first dc, loop 1 into each dc to last dc, 1 dc into last dc, turn.

Row 2 Ch 1 (does not count as st), 1 dc into each st to end, turn.

These 2 rows form patt.

Cont in patt until Rug measures 38 in. (97 cm), ending after a RS row. Fasten off. Weave in yarn ends.

FINISHING

Do not press. Carefully cut each loop to form furry effect.

This rug would also be ideal in a powder room.

Springtime Table Topper

Lacy motifs and fine cotton are combined to make this delicate table runner. Choose a color for the flowers to complement your home décor—or use lots of different hues to create a virtual flower bed. The motifs are quick and easy to make.

★★

Skill level: INTERMEDIATE

MEASUREMENTS

13 × 36½ in. (33 × 93 cm)

MATERIALS

- 2 × 50 g (1¾ oz.) balls of Rowan Cotton Glacé in Ecru 725 (A)

- 1 × 50 g (1¾ oz.) ball of Rowan Cotton Glacé in In The Pink 819 (B)

- 1 × 50 g (1¾ oz.) ball Rowan Cotton Glacé in Shoot 814 (C)

- E/4 (3.50 mm) crochet hook

GAUGE

Basic Motif measures 4 in. (10 cm) square using E/4 (3.50 mm) hook. Change hook size, if necessary, to obtain this gauge.

ABBREVIATIONS

dc2tog—*yoh and insert hook as indicated, [yoh and draw loop through] twice, rep from * once more, yoh and draw through all 3 loops on hook.

dc3tog—*yoh and insert hook as indicated, [yoh and draw loop through] twice, rep from * twice more, yoh and draw through all 4 loops on hook.

See also page 11.

BASIC MOTIF (make 27)

Using B, ch 6 and join with a ss to form a ring.

Round 1 (RS) Ch 3 (does not count as st), dc2tog into ring, (ch 3, dc3tog into ring) 7 times, ch 3, ss to top of dc2tog at beg of round. Fasten off.

With RS facing, join A into any ch sp and cont as follows:

Round 2 Ch 1 (does not count as st), 1 sc into ch sp where yarn was rejoined, *ch 5, 1 sc into next ch sp, rep from * to end, replacing sc at end of last rep with ss to first sc. Fasten off.

With RS facing, join C into any ch sp and cont as follows:

Round 3 Ch 1 (does not count as st), 1 sc into ch sp where yarn was rejoined, *ch 5, (dc3tog, ch 3, and dc3tog) into next ch sp, ch 5, 1 sc into next ch sp, rep from * to end, replacing sc at end of last rep with ss to first sc. Fasten off.

With RS facing, rejoin A into a 5-ch sp directly after a dc3tog and cont as follows:

Round 4 Ch 1 (does not count as st), 1 sc into ch sp where yarn was rejoined, *ch 5, 1 sc into next ch sp, ch 5, (1 sc, ch 5, and 1 sc) into next ch sp (this is the 3-ch sp between pairs of dc3tog)**, ch 5, 1 sc into next ch sp, rep from * to end, ending last rep at **, ch 2, 1 dc into first sc.

Round 5 Ch 1 (does not count as st), 1 sc into ch sp partly formed by dc at end of previous round, *(ch 5, 1 sc into next ch sp) twice, ch 5, (1 sc, ch 5, and 1 sc) into corner ch sp, ch 5, 1 sc into next ch sp, rep from * to end, replacing sc at end of last rep with ss to first sc.

Fasten off.

Basic Motif is a square—in each corner there is a ch sp, and there are another 4 ch sps on each side. Join Motifs while working Round 5, by replacing each (ch 5) with (ch 2, 1sc into corresponding ch sp of adjacent Motif, ch 2).

Join 27 Basic Motifs to form a rectangle 3 Motifs wide and 9 Motifs long.

Edging

With RS facing, rejoin A into one ch sp along outer edge of joined Motifs and cont as follows: ch 1 (does not count as st), 1 sc into ch sp where yarn was rejoined, *ch 6, 1 ss into 4th ch from hook, ch 2, 1 sc into next ch sp (or joined corner), rep from * all around, working twice into corner ch sps and replacing sc at end of last rep with ss to first sc.

Fasten off.

Weave in yarn ends.

FINISHING

Press carefully, following instructions on yarn label.

YARN SUPPLIERS

IN THE UNITED STATES

Accordis Acrylic Fibers
15720 John J. Delaney Dr.
Suite 204
Charlotte, NC 28277-2747
www.courtelle.com

Berroco, Inc
Elmdale Rd.
Uxbridge, MA 01569
Tel: (508) 278-2527

Boye Needle/Wrights
South St.
W.Warren, MA 01092
www.wrights.com

Brown Sheep Co., INC.
100662 Country Rd. 16
Scottsbluff, NE 69361
Tel: (308) 635-2198

Cherry Tree Hill Yarn
52 Church St.
Barton, VT 05822
Tel: (802) 525-3311

Coats & Clark
Consumer Services
P.O. Box 12229
Greeneville, SC 29612-0224
Tel: (800) 648-1479
www.coatsandclark.com

Dale of Norway, Inc.
6W23390 Stonebridge Dr.,
Waukesha, WI 53186
Tel: (262) 544-1996

Elite Yarns
300 Jackson St.
Lowell, MA 01852
Tel: (978) 453-2837

Herrschners Inc.
2800 Hoover Rd.
Stevens Point, WI 54481
www.herrschners.com

JCA Inc.
35 Scales Lane
Townsend, MA 01469
Tel: (978) 597-3002

Knitting Fever Inc.
PO Box 502
Roosevelt, NY 11575
Tel: (516) 546-3600
www.knittingfever.com

Knit Picks
13118 NE 4th St.
Vancouver, WA 98684
Tel: (800) 574-1323
www.knitpicks.com

Lion Brand Yarn Co.
34 West 15th St.
New York, NY 10011
Tel: (212) 243-8995
www.lionbrand.com

Patternworks
P.O. Box 1618
Center Harbor, NH 03226
Tel: (800) 723-9210
www.patternworks.com

Personal Threads
8025 West Dodge Rd.
Omaha, NE 68114
Tel: (800) 3306-7733
www.personalthreads.com

Red Heart ® Yarns
Two Lakepointe Plaza
4135 So. Stream Blvd.
Charlotte, NC 28217
www.coatsandclark.com

Rowan USA
4 Townsend West, Suite 8
Nashua, NH 03063
Tel: (603) 886-5041/5043
Email: wfibers@aol.com
www.knitrowan.com

Solutia/Acrilan ® Fibers
320 Interstate N. Pkwy.
Suite 500
Atlanta, GA 30339
www.themartyarns.com

TMA Yarns
206 W. 140th St.
Los Angeles, CA 90061

Trendsetter Yarns
16742 Stagg St.
Van Nuys, CA 91406
Tel: (818) 780-5497

Unique Kolours
23 North Bacton Hill Rd.
Malvern, PA 19355
Tel: (610) 280-7720
Fax: (610) 280-7701
www.uniquekolours.com

Yarns and ...
26440 Southfield Rd.
Lower Level #3
Lathrup Village, MI 48076-4551
Tel: (800) 520-YARN
www.yarns-and.com

IN CANADA

A la Tricoteuse
779 Rachel Est
Montreal
Tel: (514) 527–2451

Baadeck Yarns
16 Chebucto St.
Baadeck
Tel: (902) 295–2993

Beehave Wool Shop
2207 Oak Bay Ave.
Victoria
Tel: (250) 598–2272

Birch Hill Yarns
417–12445 Lake Fraser Dr. SE
Calgary
Tel: (403) 271–4042

Diamond Yarn
155 Martin Ross, Unit 3
Toronto, ON, M3J 2L9
Tel: (416) 736–6111
Fax: (416) 736–6112
www.diamondyarn.com

Gina Brown's
17, 6624 Centre Sr SE
Calgary
Tel: (403) 255–2200

The Knit & Stitch Shoppe
246a Marine Drive
West Vancouver
Tel: (604) 922–1023

La Dauphine
1487 Chemin Ste-Foy
Quebec City
Tel: (417) 527–3030

Passionknit Ltd.
3467 Yonge St
Toronto
Tel: (416) 322–0688

Prairie Lily Knitting & Weaving Shop
7–1730 Quebec Ave.
Saskatoon
Tel: (306) 665–2771

Ram Wools
1266 Fife Street
Winnipeg, MB, R2X 2N6
Tel: (204) 949–6868
www.ramwools.com

Saute Mouton
20 Webster St.
Lambert
Tel: (514) 671–1155

Wool Tyme
2–190 Colonnade Rd S.
Ottawa
Tel: (888) 241–7653
www.wool-tyme.com

Yarn Forward
581 Bank St
Ottawa
Tel: (877) yar–nfwd

IN AUSTRALIA

Australian Country Spinners
314 Albert Street
Brunswick
Victoria 3056
Tel: (03) 9380–3888

Creative Images
PO Box 106
Hastings
Victoria 3915
Tel: (03) 5979–1555
Fax: (03) 5979–1544
Email:
creative@peninsula.starway.net.au

Greta's Handicraft Centre
321 Pacific Highway
Lindfield
NSW 2070
Tel: (02) 9416–2489

Jo Sharp Pty Ltd
P.O. Box 357
Albany, WA 6331
Tel: (08) 9842–2250
www.josharp.com.au

Knitters of Australia
498 Hampton Street
Hampton
VIC 3188
Tel: (03) 9533–1233

Lindcraft
Gallery Level
Imperial Arcade
Pitt Street
Sydney
NSW 2000
Tel: (02) 9221–5111

Sunspun
185 Canterbury Road
Canterbury
VIC 3126
Tel: (03) 9830–1609

INDEX